Celtic Oracles

Celtic Oracles

A New System for Spiritual Growth and Divination

Rosemarie Anderson

art by
Susan Dorf

Three Rivers Press New York

Published by Three Rivers Press, 201 East 50th Street,
New York, New York 10022.
Member of the Crown Publishing Group.

Originally published in hardcover by Harmony Books, 1998.
First paperback edition printed in 2000.

Random House, Inc. New York, Toronto, London, Sydney, Auckland
www.randomhouse.com

Printed in the United States of America

Design by Lynne Amft

Library of Congress Cataloging-in-Publication Data
Anderson, Rosemarie.
Celtic oracles: a new system for spiritual growth and divination/
by Rosemarie Anderson; art by Susan Dorf.
Includes bibliographical references.
1. Oracles. 2. Mythology, Celtic—Miscellanea. I. Title.
BF1773.A53 1998
133.3—dc21 97-30944

ISBN 0-609-80275-5

10 9 8 7 6 5 4 3 2 1

First Paperback Edition

~For my parents, Mirjam Selma and Roy Goethe

CONTENTS

PREFACE

My journey for writing this book began nearly twenty years ago when I was living in Germany in a small village above the confluence of the Rhine and Neckar Rivers, once a Celtic stronghold. I was then an academic dean, ably passing as a high-functioning right-brained administrator and professor. Yet, in my private life, the timeless memory in the land spoke to me through dreams and sensations. Memories touched me, like air tendering the skin of a newborn, of an ancient time when the earth was the heart of knowing and its creatures were as familiar to one another as we might be to our friends and lovers. Animals, trees, plants, and spirits invited me to experience their reality, where nothing is lost because they remember even as we forget. This intuitive and sensuous knowledge has guided all my research in the Celtic ways.

The new oracle system introduced in this book is based on ancient Celtic symbols for the purpose of divination and spiritual growth. The introduction provides an overview of the oracle's inception and historic roots, Celtic history and worldview, the nature of divination among the Celts, as well as instructions for casting and interpreting the oracles.

I hope that you will explore this new oracle, inviting it to speak to you personally with guidance and insights that have immediate relevance to your life. The symbols of this oracle are like windows into the Celtic world. You have sixty-four of them to explore, and in time you will meet them all. Each symbol is a supernatural being or quality of the Celtic world. In encountering them, the symbols and their stories will grow and change and grace your unfolding story.

The creation of this oracle system has been guided and supported by the goodwill and talents of wonderful friends. Isaiah Williams, piper, songwriter, and natural trickster, keeps me laughing. Penelope Duckworth, poet and fellow priest, brings me hope that the church won't completely abandon me for writing this book. Jill Mellick, author and painter, inspires me to write prose well. Special thanks also go to Kay Mullin, author and harpist. In traveling together and during long stays in her home in County Donegal, Ireland, our conversations have shaped many of the stories and reflections incorporated in this book. They and other friends and family have been tirelessly supportive and encouraging. Finally, the book is dedicated to my parents for their love, courage, and refinement.

Writing a book is a labor of love. Many have contributed in specific ways. Two of Ireland's finest contemporary poets writing in Irish, Cathal Ó Searcaigh and Gabriel Rosenstock, gave assistance and encouragement—Cathal suggesting I include the Faery Lover in the oracle (the only major change in oracle since inception) and Gabriel checking the Gaelic orthography. The librarians and staff of the Irish Folklore Department, University College Dublin, patiently guided me in using the Gaelic card catalogue and provided many authoritative suggestions as well. The Institute of Transpersonal Psychology, where I teach, has given me support and encouragement to conduct research and write. Susan Dorf, the book's illustrator, has transported mere words on paper into beautiful images. I am also especially grateful to my editors, Leslie Meredith and Laura Wood at Harmony Books, for their masterful advice and stewardship of this project.

INTRODUCTION

Carved from the Night

Imagine a way of life in which guidance is formed from the stories told and retold in the night, the images found in the silence of winters, and the whisperings of otherworldly beings hidden but quickening, a little out of sight. Like contemporary block prints, Celtic images and myths are released as if carved from the mysteries of the night.

In a time when so many of us feel a yearning to connect with the natural rhythms of the earth and of our own lives—our awakenings and dyings, our creativity and sorrows—more and more of us are turning to native traditions and oracular systems to solicit guidance and support. One of the most colorful and comprehensive of these indigenous traditions is found close at hand among the European Celts. Imaginative and attuned to the signs of nature, the Celts "divined" answers from the animals, plants, people, wind, and seasons. Trees and animals especially had knowledge of all things—past, present, and future. Bards, druids, holy women and men, healers, diviners for water, and particularly augurers gained their powers to see into the unseen and to heal from the natural changes and movements of the weather, animals, and people around them. The stories and legends told and refined through the generations amassed a great store of knowledge to heal, protect, and transmit wisdom.

This book distills these ancient Celtic symbols and stories into an oracle system for the contemporary reader. It is composed of sixty-four symbols from the ancient Celtic ways of knowing. The symbols represent hundreds of years (if not two or three thousand) of Celtic culture and history, derived from pre-Christian archaeology of insular (Ireland and England) and continental Europe and the myths, historical legends, folktales, and faery traditions of Ireland, Scotland, and Wales. Like windows into an ancient world, each symbol reflects a Celtic response to events and circumstances in our lives today. For those of us attracted to the Celtic imagination and merriment or with ancestral roots in Celtic lands, the symbols may resonate deeply, even wondrously, as if the long-slumbering symbols are quickening once again. Use them to convey guidance to the circumstances and questions in your life and to glimpse a Celtic vision of the world.

Who Were the Celts?

The Celtic civilization emerged in about 900 B.C. from the remnants of the goddess-based cultures of Old Europe (6500–3500 B.C.) and exists into the present time on its most western fringe—Ireland, Wales, and Scotland—and to a lesser extent in Cornwall and Brittany. While coalescing as a culture, small, isolated groups formed tribal groups who lived in the dark forests that once virtually covered the European continent north of the Alps. The prominence of mother, bird, and snake goddesses revered by the early Celts attests to their close lineage from the matrifocal goddess cultures of Old Europe masterfully documented by the late archaeologist Marija Gimbutas.[1] The religious iconography from these early periods reveals the authority of the goddesses, the sovereign mothers who signify creation through birth and abundance and, through their many gifts, life and inspiration.

In increasing numbers, the Bronze and Iron Age Celts cultivated and hunted the plenteous and fertile river valleys of northern Europe—the Danube, Rhine, Elbe, Rhone, and their tributaries. By the fourth century B.C., Celtic tribes had expanded along the river valleys in search of new and fertile lands. Gradually moving north along the Rhine and across the North Sea to England, south along the Rhone to the Mediterranean and Spain, and east along the Danube to the Balkans and Turkey, the tribes encountered and challenged the authority of Athens, and later Rome. By then they had developed strong tribal systems and a distinct and unifying language, culture, and artistry. Dynamic and well armed, the Celts soon controlled much of inhabited Europe north of the Alps, occupying modern France, Germany, Holland, Belgium, Luxembourg, Switzerland, and Austria, as well as northern Italy and Spain, much of the Balkans, and even parts of Turkey, known then as Galatia. The intricate decorations of the gilt silver Gundestrup Cauldron (Nationalmuseet, Copenhagen) attests to the expanse of the Celtic tribes in Europe. While found in Jutland in Denmark, the cauldron may have been crafted as far south as the Balkans, in the second, third, or fourth century B.C.

Feared in Athens and Rome for the power of their swift-moving armies and curse-rendering druids, the Celts flourished through the turn of the millennium and into the first and second centuries in central Europe. Then the Roman armies began to move north. Initially under the leadership of Julius Caesar, they invaded Celtic territories, first conquering the Celts in the Po River valley of northern Italy, then the Celtic territories of modern-day Switzerland, France, and Germany. Gradually conquering one tribe at a time, Rome controlled all of central Europe and most of the British Isles by the end of the second century.

Only Ireland and the rugged highlands of Wales and Scotland—remote and inaccessible—were spared the devastating swath of the Roman armies and culture. Brittany, in the northwestern corner of France, and Cornwall, in southwestern England, though militarily conquered, were neither continuously occupied nor dominated by Rome. Never occupied by Roman armies or assimilated into a Roman and Mediterranean culture and worldview, the Irish Celts and Celtic highlanders of Wales and Scotland continued their traditions without encumbrance—even from the Roman Church—well into the fourth century.

Initially, Christianity came to Ireland and Wales by way of seafaring merchants spreading "the new religion of the east" more than through emissaries from the official church. Blending indigenous traditions with the new religion, a unique form of Celtic Christianity developed, especially in Ireland, Scotland, and Wales. In Ireland, the historic encounter was extraordinary, sparking a renaissance in art and literature. The undermining of this creative and lively Christianity is one of the saddest stories of European history. By the end of the seventh century, the religious authority of Rome had repudiated Celtic traditions everywhere. What survived was hidden from authorities and disguised in seemingly harmless stories and practices among country people.

The Celtic Worldview

For several hundred years, the Celts of central and Alpine Europe had been a pastoral and agrarian people, unmolested by the city cultures of the Greek and Roman empires rimming the Mediterranean Sea. Traveling bards and village storytellers and singers transmitted lore, clan lineage, and wisdom. Priestly authorities, such as druids, shamans, and healers, practiced ritual and alchemical healing and apprenticed younger men and women in their arts. Knowledge of medicine and herbs, law and ethical codes, and tribal traditions, as well as psychological and spiritual wisdom was recorded in vibrant and rhythmical verse. All of life—each season with its message, the flight of the birds at the hour of a child's birth, the spontaneous nuances to a well-known story, and an unexpected happening in a familiar place—gave sacred semblance and direction to ordinary life events. If people were wise enough to read the signs, every moment was oracular, a prophecy amid the press of time. Life moved from the ordinary to the sacred in a never-ending cycle, a cycle we are beginning to rediscover in our own time.

Living in a storytelling and mythic world, the Celts saw that all aspects of life were greatly interconnected. The oracles in this divination system were likewise connected, one to another. The Triple-Mother Goddess (Oracle 1), for example, represents the sovereign goddess in all her aspects—maiden, mother, and crone. Oracle 7, the Snake and Fire Goddess Brigit, is also a mother goddess, but her special aspect in this oracle is her power to convey transformation, specialized in her concern for midwifery, blacksmithing, and fostering the creative arts. The Cauldron of Creation of Oracle 2 is signified by an inexhaustible cauldron from which all the creatures of the earth flow. The voluptuous and sensuous authority of sovereignty itself, manifested in all the goddesses in varying degrees, is singularly addressed in Oracle 33, while the Hag (Oracle 5) is the Initiator, a wise woman who appears as both young and old. In distinguishing the goddess's many unique aspects, her primal authority is apparent.

An important mythic configuration is Brigit's as the Snake Goddess, the Ram-horned Snake (Oracle 23), and the Banishing of Snakes by St. Patrick in Ireland (Oracle 24). This configuration represents the historic transition from a matrifocal goddess tradition to a patrifocal warrior tradition. Snakes have signified transformation and have been associated with the goddess since Neolithic times. In the Celtic tradition, Brigit is associated with snakes more than any other goddess. Once the bitterness of winter is spent, Brigit is celebrated as a snake emerging from the ground in early February to signal the beginning of spring. The Ram-horned Snake represents transformation in the aspect of shape-shifting. By tradition, however, St. Patrick is responsible for banishing snakes from Ireland from atop a summit sacred to the mother goddesses. St. Patrick banishes a snakelike monster sometimes called the devil's mother. By legend, the goddesses are symbolically exiled and replaced by a superior strength personified in a heroic, demon-fighting St. Patrick.

Wherever the Celts lived, their world was altogether lively and connected with a sensitivity toward a magical Otherworld. Located beneath the surface of the earth or on blessed isles far to the west (Oracle 64), the

Otherworld is the special habitat of the faeries, ancestors, gods, and most especially the goddesses who gave the land its power and the plants their natural fluorescence. In mythic history, a godlike race known as the Tuatha Dé Danann, the People of the Goddess Danu, inhabited Ireland prior to the coming of the Celts. From them the Celts perfected the arts of magic and druidry. Still today, the Tuatha Dé live in Ireland, but beneath the ground as supernatural beings or faeries, appearing on earth only occasionally, such as on Samhain (Halloween) to mark the beginning of winter and Beltaine (May Eve) to mark the beginning of summer. On these nights the veils between the realms are their thinnest, allowing faeries and humans to pass easily between the realms.

For the Celts, the animals, the land's features, the earth, and the sky were spirit beings as well as physical manifestations. Animals were revered not only as sources of sustenance and labor but for their animal nature and the spirit of the animal that mirrored the Otherworld so purely. The Celts honored the land and the natural energies that percolated up from the earth's vast interior. The landscape was animated by otherworldly presences. Each glen, river, spring at its source, mountain, and estuary had a special power, utterly unique and powerful. Especially attuned to these energies, the Celts, like other native peoples globally, built their sacred places, their settlements, and homes in power places where they felt assurance of blessing and protection from the ancestors and supernatural beings of the Otherworld.

Adding to their vast store of knowledge from the subtleties of everyday experience, storytellers and bards kept the ancient traditions alive. Storytellers and bards were welcomed and revered. Their charms protected the people from illness and injury. In reverse, their curses—often in the form of deadly satire—confounded the enemy and sometimes inflicted death. Even in our time, poetry and prose flourish in Celtic countries, especially in Ireland where the eccentricities of poets are enjoyed, not just tolerated, by the public. Indeed, Gaelic poetry reveals not only the lyricism of Gaelic languages (even when it is the background to speaking in English) but the sweet blend of the ancient myth and legend and contemporary writing.

Divination

Many ancient systems of divination are found worldwide. Among the most well known are the Tarot, from medieval Europe, with origins possibly in Egypt and the Near East, and the *I Ching* or *Book of Changes* from China, and its strong Confucian and Taoist interpretations. Recently, Ralph H. Blum in *The Book of Runes* has reintroduced the runes as a contemporary oracle; their last known use was in medieval Iceland. Whether influenced by divine will or the unconscious human mind, the casting of lots, the throwing of yarrow sticks, or the arraying of special cards have yielded both simple answers or complex symbols in need of interpretation—outcomes thought to be inspired and prophetic.

Within Western traditions, divination has played a paradoxical role over the centuries in Judaism, Christianity, and Islam. Fortune-telling and magic have often been forbidden by religious law. Various forms of divination have nonetheless been popular and even favored at various times as a means of discerning the will of God. In the plaintive story of Samuel and his son Jonathan in 1 Samuel 14:36–45, Jonathan's guilt is discovered by the casting of lots, perhaps small sticks or dice, an oracle known as "urim and thummim." Other references to urim and thummim are found in scripture written prior to the exile in Babylon, as well as more symbolic references written during the period of the return to Israel and the restoration of the temple in Jerusalem.[2] In Acts 1:23–26, the apostle Judas is replaced by Mathias by the casting of lots.

Among the ancient Celts, archaeological evidence indicates an early fascination with visions and prophesy. Ravens (Oracle 19) depicted on cave walls in the Camonica Valley of northern Italy by Bronze and Iron Age Celts are portrayed as though speaking to humans to give guidance and prophesy. Throughout Irish legend and mythic history, ravens are ominous prognosticators, usually forecasting death and carnage in the battle ahead. Small sun symbols (Oracle 63) were buried with the dead, as though to convey light and vision and extend prophesy into realms beyond this earthly life.

Celtic Christianity and Divination

The most extraordinary example of divination among Celtic people is found in the writing of Alexander Carmichael. Traveling throughout the Outer Hebrides and the Highlands of Scotland as a civil servant in the late nineteenth century, he lovingly recorded the prayers, songs, and practices of the cotters and crofters. Carmichael notes that divination or augury was commonly practiced among the people, though hidden from the clergy, who were fiercely opposed to the practice. Divination concerned revealing the whereabouts and condition of people and animals who were absent and could not be seen or known about by ordinary means. The gift of augury, like second sight or seeing into the faery realms, was inherited, though often was known to skip a generation and pass to one family member and not another. Carmichael wrote:

> *The augury was made on the first Monday of the quarter and immediately before sunrise. The augurer, fasting, and with bare feet, bare head, and closed eyes, went to the doorstep and placed a hand on each jamb. Mentally beseeching the God of the unseen to show him his quest and to grant him his augury, the augurer opened his eyes and looked steadfastly straight in front of him. From the nature and position of the objects within his sight, he drew his conclusions.*[3]
>
> *The signs are many and varied. [For example,] A man standing, or a beast rising, indicates that the person who is the*

> *object of the quest is casting off the sickness from which he had been suffering. . . . A man lying down indicates sickness. . . . A beast lying down indicates death. A woman, in particular a fair, brown, or black woman, is fortunate, and a woman standing is very good. . . . A cock coming or looking towards the seer is excellent. A bird approaching indicates news. . . . Fowls without a cock . . . especially if approaching . . . are harmful. Still worse is the raven, especially if approaching: it is a sign of death.*[4]

According to the traditions recorded by Alexander Carmichael, auguries were dedicated to either the Virgin Mary or St. Brigit (also known as the Bride; a vestige of the goddess Brigit in Oracle 7). When the young Jesus was nowhere to be found, Mary made an augury by making a tube with the palms of her hands and looking through them saw Jesus in the temple disputing with the elders.[5] When Jesus was again absent, Mary asked Brigit to make an augury in order to find him. As Mary did earlier, she made a tube with her hands and looking through them saw Jesus sitting beside a well.[6] Therefore, divination was known in old Scotland as the Augury of Mary or the Augury of Brigit. Along with the augurers of Outer Hebrides, you might like to say this simple prayer of invocation before casting your oracle:

Augury of Mary

God over me, God under me,
God before me, God behind me,
I on Thy path, O God,
Thou, O God, in my steps.

The augury made of Mary to her Son,
The offering made of Bride through her palm,
Sawest Thou it, King of life?—
Said the King of life that He saw.

The augury made by Mary for her own offspring,
When He was for a space amissing,
Knowledge of truth, not knowledge of falsehood,
That I shall truly see all my quest.

Son of beauteous Mary, King of life,
Give Thou me eyes to see all my quest,
With grace that shall never fail, before me,
That shall never quench nor dim.[7]

Creating This Oracle

This oracle was created on a quiet Sunday afternoon. For many months, a family crisis had interrupted my writing and research in Celtic archaeology, mythology, literature, art, and music. At last, a leisurely afternoon stretched before me. In twenty minutes, I sketched out the essentials of a new oracle system. Emerging in a flash of insight, the system seemed already formed and nourished by the silent months just past. Feeling utterly alive and refreshed, my scholarly sensibilities crossed into the realms of the otherworldly and oracular.

Each of the sixty-four oracles in this new system represents a symbol that stretches back through centuries of Celtic history. Whether a goddess or sacred animal, each symbol has a long historical lineage often dating back to the dawn of Celtic culture and artistry. In recent years, archaeological findings and consequent understanding of early Celtic religious life allow for situating Celtic mythology (largely dating from early or middle medieval periods) and more recent folklore traditions into a larger cultural context. For example, the horse goddess Epona (Oracle 8) figures prominently in the bas-relief statuary of the Roman-Celtic period. As sovereign and goddess, Epona was revered throughout insular and continental Europe by native Celts and Roman soldiers, especially cavalrymen garrisoned in Celtic lands. In Irish and Welsh mythology, she appears as the horse goddess Macha and Rhiannon, respectively. Similarly, figures of supernatural boars and pigs (Oracle 17) made by Iron Age Celts are depicted realistically, though with exaggerated horns and ferocious features. In Welsh legends in particular, boars are extolled as sacred animals, gifts from the Otherworld to humans living in the Middle World between the subterranean Otherworld and the sky. These connections, both readily apparent and subtle, are documented in the historical section for each oracle. Whenever possible, I have also used folklore and modern poetry to illustrate the continuity of tradition.

Choosing the symbols for this new system of divination occurred spontaneously. However, I was implicitly guided by my ongoing discoveries in Celtic culture and history. As I stated earlier, archaeological, mythological, and folkloric evidence indicates that the early Celts represented the remnants of an earlier, goddess-based European culture called Old Europe. In statuary, largely from the first few centuries A.D., goddesses are every bit as unique and prominent as gods, if not more so. When partnered, Celtic goddesses and gods appear in bas relief images as equals. Similarly, in mythic tales from later periods, goddesses and queen warriors are as lively, sexual, and ferocious as are gods and champions. If anything, gods and heroes seem more like one another in attributes than the goddesses and heroines. Cerwidwen the Hag (Oracle 5) and the goddesses Morrigán, Brigit, and Epona (Oracles 6–9) are distinct and lively personalities—much more so than the Sky God, Taranis, Oengus, or Lugh (Oracles 57–60), who largely fight and conquer, though some heroes, such as Cú Chulainn of the Ulster Cycle, are well-developed characters. The women are more vital and persuasive as personalities, signifying the strength of their lineage from ancient times. Over time, as is well known, the goddess-based foundation of early Celtic culture was gradually superseded by a warrior-based tradition largely orchestrated by the actions of gods, kings, and fighters of various sorts. By early medieval times, the role of women was greatly diminished and heroines banished to myth or revered as Christian saints, who could be more safely honored from afar.

One additional consideration begs mentioning. An informed Celtic reader might wonder, for example, why I have included only four trees in this oracle system (Oracles 25–28) when many trees were held sacred by the Celts. I have chosen trees that are unique and prominent in Celtic lore. If I had included every tree possible, this system would be largely composed of trees. You might want to acquaint yourself with the trees in your own natural environment, using the descriptions of the temperate zone trees in this system, not only as oracles giving guidance, but as starting places to learn about the sacred properties of the trees where you live. In the same way, the animals and nature spirits in your environment may be quite different than the ones in this system. Get to know them as allies.

How to Cast This Oracle

The sixty-four Celtic oracles contained in this book are symbols conveying the power and wisdom of the ancient Celtic way of knowing. The symbols are gracious and healing. By casting this oracle, the symbols bring you a wider spiritual perspective and insight into the unconscious forces within your nature that shape your actions, habits, and ways of thinking. Without a clear awareness of the spiritual and unconscious forces motivating you, your life can seem especially out of control and bewildering. The oracle allows you to see patterns and possibilities you might otherwise overlook, dismiss, or deny. Consulting the oracle is not fortune-telling in the conventional sense. It will not tell you what job to take, who to marry, which automobile to buy, or whether you should travel to India or Hawaii this year. It may, however, give you insight into the unseen motives directing your choices. It may widen your perspective, allowing you to glimpse the pervasive spiritual forces at work in your life. It may help you to see behind the sometimes confusing circumstances of your life, thereby calming your fears and supporting your health and well-being. Inevitably, the oracle will invite you to make superior choices and act in accord with the best possible outcome for yourself and others.

Depending on your spiritual tradition (or the lack of one), it is usually best to consult the oracle after a period of meditation, prayer, or reflection. A respectful attitude allows for more possibilities in everyday life, and so it is in the spirit world as well. In consulting the oracle, take your time, relax, reflect on your life circumstances or puzzlement, and consider how best to word a question. You might wish to ritualize the practice in some way by going to a favorite place, using a special set of coins to cast oracles, or recording your questions and answers in a journal or special book used only for this purpose.

Because this oracle system seeks to see the unknown patterns behind the circumstances of your life, it is usually best to ask questions about a specific situation and invite the most significant possible response or answer from the oracle. Your particular life situation is unique and personal, but the spirit world abounds with possibilities. Vague questions convey vague answers, because it is difficult to know to whom or what a symbol might refer in interpretation. The oracle may even bypass or circumvent simple either/or questions, giving an answer about inner motives instead. Ask questions about the inherent nature of a particular situation or the purpose behind a particular relationship, and then bid the oracle to comment freely. Once the question is clear in your mind, write it down. You may wish to say the Augury of Mary given earlier in this Introduction as an invocation.

To cast the oracle you need two coins. Any two coins will do, but special coins used only for casting will help you focus and establish your personal connection with the oracle, especially when you are hurried or otherwise distracted. Before casting the coins, establish one side as "heads" and the other as "tails." Throw the first coin, and record whether it turns up heads or tails. Then, throw the second coin, recording heads or tails. You will get one of four possible combinations. If you get two heads, the number is 1. If you get two tails, the number is 2. If you first cast heads and second tails, the number is 3. If you first cast tails and second heads, the number is 4. Record the number after your question. The values are shown here:

First Throw	Second Throw	Number Assigned
Heads	Heads	1
Tails	Tails	2
Heads	Tails	3
Tails	Heads	4

You will repeat this process two more times, recording each number. In casting the two coins a total of three times, you will get one of sixty-four combinations of numbers. Oracle 1, the Triple-Mother Goddess, for example, is cast by throwing heads-heads, heads-heads, and heads-heads consecutively—or 1, 1, and 1. Oracle 64, Tír na nÓg (the Blessed Isle to the West), is cast by throwing tails-tails, tails-tails, and tails-tails consecutively—or 4, 4, and 4. Appendix B lists all possible number sequences and their equivalent oracle.

Interpreting the Oracles

All sixty-four oracles in this system are interrelated. They come from a Celtic worldview in which narrative and story is the web of everyday life. Some of these interconnections were described earlier, but you are likely to find many others. With practice in using the oracle, the interrelatedness of the oracles will allow you to understand more fully the Celtic worldview and enrich your understanding of each oracle in the process.

Having cast the oracle, the oracle's meaning and application to your life may be immediately obvious, or it may take time to unravel its meaning and application. Oracles based on ancient symbols such as these have both obvious and subtle layers of meaning. If you immediately grasp the significance of the oracle in answering your question, how fortunate, although you may, over time, find more subtle meanings and new dimensions. Sometimes an oracle may at first seem puzzling or unintelligible. Taking time to reflect on the oracle's meaning and watching for similar symbols in your immediate environment, everyday reading, or news from friends may bring greater depth to your understanding. You may see symbols and images you never noticed before. You may even feel as though the symbols want to jump off the page and converse, creating an interpretation all your own. It is therefore especially helpful to let your imagination roam, inviting the personalities and stories in the oracles to have a life of their own.

From time to time, you may wonder why the oracle appears not to be answering your question. When and if this happens, there are at least two possible interpretations. Perhaps finding the answer gradually and developing it along the way is more supportive of your best interests. The answer you received may be a temporary or partial one, and you may have to ask again later. The oracle may simply be waiting for a more opportune time, when taking action will be more auspicious. The other interpretation is that the oracle is circumventing your particular question and addressing a more essential issue in your life. Perhaps you have asked the wrong question. The answer you received may actually be unsolicited guidance on an issue more important or crucial than the question you have asked. The Morrigán (Oracle 6), which signifies chaos and confusion, can also be interpreted as the oracle not wishing to answer a particular question at this time.

Frequently, the same oracle or related oracles come up again and again, even in response to different questions. If so, watch for that symbol mirroring many aspects of your life. A basic issue, represented by one or more related oracles, may have overriding significance in your life at this time. For example, you might repeatedly cast one or several manifestations of the goddess in response to a variety of questions, signifying integration of certain of her aspects. Alternatively, you might cast the oracle for Cernunnos, Antlered God of the Animals (Oracle 21), or Cernunnos and Utterly Stag (Oracle 22) and Sacred King (Oracle 14) repeatedly. If so, the configuration of issues of authority, taking responsibility for your actions, and harnessing the passions of your own nature may be essential for evolving personal and spiritual growth. Also, several oracles (Oracles 6, 37, and 48) are related to sensuality, intimacy, and eroticism. Frequently drawing these oracles suggests a need to consider your needs for personal intimacy with others in several aspects of your life. Repeatedly casting faery oracles (Oracles 45–48), on the other hand, may indicate an attraction to whimsical and artistic realms of spirit signified by the otherworldly faeries. Always, this oracle system is dynamic. Allow it to work for you.

Having gleaned the basic meaning of an oracle, you may expect to draw the aspects of the symbol into your life in the days and weeks ahead. The Morrigán (Oracle 6) may unexpectedly appear, for example, as your adolescent daughter throwing chaos and sexuality into your life. The Mother Goddess Carrying Children and Food (Oracle 3) may be found in aspects of your dreams, in the qualities you now admire in the people around you, and in the advertisements that attract you and the products you buy. The trickster Pooka (Oracle 43) may appear as a series of baffling events or trivial but exasperating accidents. The Faeries of Mischief and Humor (Oracle 46) may be your teasing younger brother or an annoying but benevolent colleague. It is also possible to actively bring the symbol into your life. Whether mythic personalities, trees, elemental nature spirits, gods, or goddesses, there are practical ways to attract and explore their qualities. For example, if you draw the oracle of the New Moon (Oracle 53), you may wish to take more walks under the moonlight or meditate outdoors. If you draw one of the tree oracles (Oracles 25–28) or animal oracles (Oracles 9–12 and 17–20), you may want to seek out the trees or animals in your natural environment, spend time in their presence, read about them, and reflect on their qualities. If you draw Wells and Sulfur Springs (Oracle 38), you may wish to locate a natural spring, find ways to spend more time around water, or perhaps add a fountain or Jacuzzi to your home. You are only as limited as your imagination.

Remember that in interpreting each oracle you have the opportunity to further explore the subtleties of your nature and life circumstances as well as refine your intuition. An oracle conveys insights that provide a glimpse behind the veils of what you already know. The interpretation is personal and ultimately uniquely your own.

time at the [illegible] sacred [illegible] Earlier or [illegible] Fountain, Wells and Sacred Springs (Card 37), you may seek to locate a natural spring, and wish to spend some time around water, or perhaps add a fountain or jacuzzi to your home. Your guidance is limited by your imagination.

Remember that in interpreting each oracle you have the opportunity to further explore the subtleties of your reading and the circumstances as well as refine your intuition. An oracle conveys messages that provide glimpses behind the veil of what you already know. The interpretation is personal and ultimately uniquely your own.

Part One

Oracles of the Dark Goddess

Those oracles relating to:

The Goddess and Her Attributes

The Dark Goddess of Change

The Dark Goddess and Her Animals

Sacred Union

~ I ~

Triple-Mother Goddess

MAGNIFICENCE

Invoking the Qualities of Majesty and Generativity

The Triple-Mother Goddess signifies the magnificence of mother earth in the giving of life. She presides over giving birth, the fluorescence and fruitfulness of plants, generativity at all ages, and the splendor of earthy and womanly wisdom. Though the mature wisdom of the aged woman is especially revered, she encompasses all ages, polarities, and expressions. Her qualities are majesty, generativity, and an inner connection with the life-giving sovereignty of the earth.

According to mythic history, when the Celts arrived on the shores of Ireland, they encountered the three sovereign mother goddesses, Ériu, Banba, and Fódla, who shielded and protected the land from harm. Each required the invaders to promise that if successful in occupying the land, the land would forever bear her name.

> *They had colloquy with Ériu in Uisnech. She said unto them: Warriors, said she, welcome to you. Long have soothsayers had [knowledge of] your coming. Yours shall be this island forever; and to the east of the world there shall not be a better island. No race shall there be, more numerous than yours. Good is that, said Amorgen; good is the prophecy. . . . A gift to me, ye sons of Míl, and ye children of Breogan, said she, that my name shall be on this island.*[8]

The Triple-Mother Goddess gives life to the land and its people. She preserves them from misfortune, injury, and danger. In her fiercest aspect, she is a warrior goddess wreaking havoc and death on intruders. Her motherliness more typically presides in the birthing of new forms of life and the nourishing and germinating of the land's flowers and vegetation. In locations as distant as Scotland and Hungary, and especially prevalent along the Rhone, Mosel, and Rhine river valleys of central Europe, carvings and sculptures of the Triple-Mother Goddess are remarkably alike. Typically she carries children, fruit, wine goblets, cornucopiae or trays loaded with the fruits of the harvest.

Often the Triple-Mother Goddess manifests as a maiden, mother, and crone. One or two of the goddess figures is youthful with smooth skin and rounded cheeks and another is aged with creased cheeks and a wrinkled neck. At other times, their ages are much alike but their faces different in temperament. In the Roman-occupied areas of Germany, the three mother goddesses were consistently portrayed as a central goddess who is young with long, flowing hair, carries fruit, and is surrounded on both sides by older goddesses with large, circular headdresses made of supple willow branches covered with linen. With obvious dignity and stature, she gives the impression of unquestioned authority and magnificence.

IF YOU ARE DRAWN TO THIS ORACLE, you are invited to bring authority, stability, and vitality into your personal life and affairs. Your expression and activities may need to realign with the abundance of the Triple-Mother Goddess, the life-giving and sustaining power of the earth. Her powers are sublime and primal, rooted in the earth.

In some ways you may feel unrooted, disconnected from the spontaneous fruitfulness of the natural world. The generative powers of the Triple-Mother Goddess will help lend a sense of majesty, authority, and ease to your intentions and actions. In aligning yourself with her spontaneous outpouring of energy, you will begin to reconnect your own life force with her expressions in others around you. Since the Triple Goddess faces in all directions, Her qualities are especially abundant in the natural environment and in the creatures that inhabit the earth. Spending time outdoors in nature enjoying her manifestations will help you to recharge.

~ 2 ~

Cauldron of Creation

SOURCE

Invoking the Quality of Repose and Replenishment

The goddess is the source of life and her womb the cauldron of creation giving birth to the world. Through her, all life comes into form. In Irish and Welsh legends and iconography, her womb is symbolized by the ever-replenishing cauldron of the Otherworld, always filled with savory meats for feasting and restoring dead warriors to life. Through the womb of the goddess, life is replenished with vitality from an ageless and inexhaustible source.

Life begins in the womb of the goddess. Ceaselessly, she births the Milky Way. The stars, moon, planets, trees and plants, animals, people, and all that is yet to exist issue from her womb. From an enormous force within, life spews forth, magnificently, hugely, intensely, and relentlessly. No god, no man or woman can tame this rite of passage. Like the mythic cauldron that symbolizes her womb, life tempestuously brews.

Yet, men and women try to ease the advancing passage. In a poem entitled "Mór Hatching," originally written in Gaelic, contemporary Irish poet Nuala Ní Dhomhnaill addresses the age-old mother with all the awe and ambivalence of an ancient Celt:

I'm telling you,
unruly Mór,
that green snakes
will emanate from your womb
if you stay hatching
out this poisoned kernel
one day more.

Gather to yourself,
like a bee,
the hours that are blossoming
in the sun's sharp sting:
they ripen in the heat.

Gather them—
from them create
honeyed days.[9]

On the Gundestrup Cauldron, one of the prominent side plates portrays a large figure, probably divine, standing before a procession of Celtic warriors. One by one, the deity appears to dip and remove them from the cauldron, as though to restore them to life.[10] Irish and Welsh folktales tell of enchanted pots and bowls ever full of meal or tasty brew.

In the Tale of Branwen from the Second and Third Branch of the *Mabinogion*, Matholwch, an Irish king, sails to Wales, and hoping to form an alliance, approaches Bendigeidfran, son of Llfr, the king of Wales. When Matholwch is hideously insulted by an outraged chieftain, the king's half-brother, Bendigeidfran, appeases his anger by giving him a gift above price, a magic cauldron.

> *I will give you a cauldron with a special property: should a man of yours be killed today, cast him into the cauldron, and by tomorrow he will be as good as ever but he will be without speech.*[11]

IF YOU ARE DRAWN TO THIS ORACLE, you may be feeling weary or inwardly depleted. This oracle calls for repose, rest, and a complete overhaul of life energies before energy and vitality are replenished. While the goddess is inexhaustible in her powers to restore, you are urged to cooperate by retreating from the activities of life. Seek solitude. Do as little as possible. Sleep. Relax. Engage in small and subtle activities that quiet rather than excite the mind. Meditate or pray. Let the mind unwind and settle naturally.

Once you are emptied of your automatic and perhaps busy life, you will begin to feel more spacious and free. If you are rested and quiet within, you may notice subtle changes in your awareness. As with any birth, beginnings may at first be unsettling and even messy. Nonetheless, in time new life will naturally arise within you. You will feel replenished, as though filled up by an unknown and timeless source.

~ 3 ~
Mother Goddess Carrying Children and Food

WELL-BEING

Invoking the Qualities of Comfort and Contentment

The mother goddess in her aspect of beneficence gives nourishment, food, and well-being to domestic life. Her mothering tends to the immediate and personal needs of daily human life. She cradles and nurses infants, is surrounded by children under her care, and carries fruits, ears of corn, grains, cakes, breads, goblets of wine, kegs, pots, baskets and cornucopiae spilling over with fruits, grains, and breads. Her dependable and soothing attention provides comfort and contentment in daily life.

Images of the mother goddess of well-being are found throughout the Celtic territories. As a local maternal sovereign, she attends to the everyday needs of life by sustaining the local crops, blessing the harvest, nursing the babies, comforting the sick and the dying, pouring out the wine, and dispensing the fruits of the harvest. The passing of life, the cycle of birth and death, and the vicissitudes of day-to-day existence are her concerns. Her presence is familiar, homey, and soothing. Amid the insecurities and dangers of life, she blesses life with comfort, constancy, and contentment.

Whether depicted as a single goddess or in groups of two or three representing her magnificence (Oracle 1), the mother goddess in her aspect of loving care carries symbols of well-being, security, and prosperity intended to bless and provide for life's daily needs. In image after image, she holds fruit, grains, ears of corn, bread, pots of honey and mead. Ordinarily, she carries babies and is encircled by toddlers and older children seeking her attention and perhaps her good counsel. In this lovely image from the Rhineland, she carries two enormous cornucopiae, signifying her bountiful presence in providing food and sustenance throughout the years.

The goddess of the home and locality is immortalized in the words of the ancient poet Amergin:

I am the womb: of every holt,
I am the blaze: on every hill,
I am the queen: of every hive,
I am the shield: for every head,
I am the tomb: of every hope.[12]

IF YOU ARE DRAWN TO THIS ORACLE, you are attracting physical and emotional comfort and well-being into your life. You may be in the midst of a challenging situation, or the mundane activities or weariness of life's struggles may be tiring or exhausting your reserves.

Drawing this oracle is a wake-up call to nourish yourself with soothing activities and relationships. A complete rest is not necessary (as in Oracle 2). Nonetheless, you are asked to focus your attention on your immediate and personal needs for comfort, nourishment, and well-being. What activities would soothe you? Is your diet supporting your life? Do the people around you give you comfort and reassurance? Is there a way to receive more physical or sexual contact and comfort? Do some people and activities unnerve you or deplete you? Even seemingly minor activities can be enormously tiring or rejuvenating. Look for patterns, especially in your home life. Write them down, even if they seem unimportant at the time. Since the mother goddess is devoted to tranquillity at home, it is especially important to consider ways to bring more ease, contentment, and security to your domestic life.

Even amid trying situations, it is possible to support your physical and emotional well-being. Small signs of joy, acts of kindness, personal prayer, meditation, and attention to diet and exercise are essential. The presence of this oracle gives hope that the nourishment and comfort you need is available in your immediate environment.

~ 4 ~

The Sacred Three

Seeing in All Directions

Invoking Awareness of the Spirit World

The tripling of supernatural figures and sacred attributes signifies the all-seeing and unifying presence of the spirit world. Triplication reaches its height in the images of the Triple-Mother Goddess. Tripling the image gives an air of magic and fervor to gods, heads, horns, phalluses, horses, and faces of supernatural figures.[13] The image of the *tricephalos* appears to look out in three directions simultaneously from a single head.

The image of the Sacred Three pervades Celtic iconography and story from the pre-Roman period on through to the predominance of the Trinity in Celtic Christianity. Sublimity and power are linked to the tripling of images and attributes. The well-known Triple Spiral was carved on stones at Newgrange by the Stone Age ancestors of the Celts. Images of the Triple-Mother Goddess (Oracle 1) abound in the pre-Roman and Roman-Celtic period. By tradition, when the first Celts invaded Ireland, they were met by the three goddesses who protected the land. Brigit (Oracle 7) is sometimes triplicated or represented as three sisters. Powerful attributes such as horns and phalluses are triplicated.

Of particular significance in this image of goddesses and gods are the triple-faced or triple-headed images from northeastern Gaul, near modern Reims, as well as a few images from the south and west of Gaul and even from as far north as Scotland and Ireland. A triple-faced image may appear as a single head with three distinct faces, sometimes blended with one dominant face and two in profile. Occasionally, the heads in juxtaposition may vary in age, one old and two representing youth, and less frequently male and female faces may be combined together. Images from modern Trier and Metz portraying the Triple-Mother Goddess appear to trample on the *tricephalos* (triple-headed) god beneath, suggesting the dominance of the mother goddess over the triple-headed god.[14]

The Celts, already linking the supernatural with the Sacred Three, took naturally to Trinitarian formulations in the early Christian period. In the *Carmina Gadelica*, Alexander Carmichael chronicles the hymns, runes, prayers, invocations, and customs of late-nineteenth-century farmers and crofters of the Scottish Highlands and the Outer Hebrides. One of the loveliest rituals invoking the Trinity is an evening ritual known as the "smooring of the fire," performed by the woman of the house:

> *Peat is the fuel of the Highlands [of Scotland] and [the Outer Hebrides]... Where wood is not obtainable the fire is kept in*

during the night. The ceremony of smooring the fire is artistic and symbolic, and is performed with loving care. The embers are evenly spread on the hearth—which is generally in the middle of the floor—and formed into a circle. This circle is then divided into three equal sections, a small boss being left in the middle. A peat is laid between each section, each peat touching the boss, which forms a common centre. The first peat is laid down in name of the God of Life, the second in name of the God of Peace, the third in name of the God of Grace. The circle is then covered over with ashes sufficient to subdue but not to extinguish the fire, in name of the Three of Light. The heap slightly raised in the centre is called "Tula nan Trí," the Hearth of the Three. When the smooring operation is complete the woman closes her eyes, stretches her hand, and softly intones one of the many formulae current for these occasions.

The sacred Three
To save,
To shield,
To surround,
The hearth,
The house,
The household,
This eve,
This night,
Oh! this eve,
This night,
And every night,
Each single night.
Amen.[15]

IF YOU ARE DRAWN TO THIS ORACLE, you are focusing too narrowly on the immediate circumstances rather than looking at the larger context and possibilities for the future. The all-seeing vision of this oracle invites you to step back from the immediate situation, to scan events as though you were looking at them from a distance, and to imagine how possible outcomes might look from a future date. This enlarged perspective will inspire confidence, focus your intention, and simplify your actions.

In a larger sense, the Sacred Three reminds you that the multiplicity of forms and events before you are actually unified, if you were to see your life from an expanded perspective. The Triple Spiral expands in all directions. The *tricephalos* sees in all directions. The Christian Trinity represents the fullness of the Divine. By cultivating a wider vision, you will come to savor a grander unity beyond all the myriad forms and events in life. Your actions will become simple and efficient as you see the interrelations in your life.

~ 5 ~
Hag, the Initiator

BEGINNINGS

Invoking Readiness for Change

In Irish myth, a ghastly hag symbolizes the sovereign goddess of Ireland in the quest for the rightful heir and king. Through her, he is joined to the land. When the hag mates with the rightful heir, she signals his sovereignty by becoming a lovely maiden. In Irish and Scottish folktales, the hag gives birth to the mountains and valleys, hills and rocks, and the various creatures of the land. The hag tests and initiates beginnings and rightful change.

The powerful hag is one of the three aspects of the Triple-Mother Goddess, the sovereign goddess of the land. Typically old and yet ageless, her terrifying appearance tests the readiness of kings and heroes. In Irish, Welsh, and Scottish legends, she enchants her "chosen" heroes with magical powers and confounds and hounds any who spurn her advances. Her shape is spine-tinglingly horrid and yet radiant, as captured in a contemporary poem, originally composed in Gaelic, by Nuala Ní Dhomhnaill:

She stood naked
in the dark,
her palms cold
like luminous fish
on my shoulders:
her hips
flashing fire
beneath the two moons
of her breasts.
        I sank my head
        in her sea-weed hair
        and bitter waves of sea
        bruised and battered me,
        our white-horse waves
        rusted to rats:
        all became empurpled.
In the morning waking
my head aching
I saw sallow scales encrusted her
and rotten teeth from the abyss
snarled at me and hissed.
I took my awl and last
and left the place fast![16]

In approaching this goddess, the Irish kings were chosen. By legend, the reign of the Uí Néill, descendants of Niall, was initiated by the blessing of the goddess of sovereignty, the hag. Though the youngest of the five sons of the king, Niall became the king of Ireland from 379–405. As the story is told in an early fifth-century manuscript, Niall and his four brothers were out hunting in the forest and were overwhelmed by thirst. One by one, each brother comes upon a pool of water guarded by a hideous hag. She offers each a drink in exchange for a kiss and each one flees at her dreadful appearance, except for Niall. He kisses the crone and makes love to her. As they kiss, the hag becomes the loveliest of maidens, her face like the radiance of the sun—none other than the goddess of sovereignty herself.[17]

Folktales in Ireland, Wales, and Scotland abound in stories about the hag, the "Mountain Mother," the "Great Old One," or the Cailleach in Gaelic. Striding across the land, she "lets fall from her skirts" the natural features and creatures of the land.[18] In Ireland, many tales tell of benevolent hags, loathsome hags, hags saved by saints from peril, and hags who turn to hares and turn back into an old neighbor woman again when caught milking the cows!

IF YOU ARE DRAWN TO THIS ORACLE, the hag may be testing your readiness for change. Her presence signals the potential for significant shifts in business and professional life, relationships, and the affairs of everyday living. New beginnings are possible. While the hag's outward appearance may be ghastly, welcoming her signals your readiness for a shift in awareness and fortunes. Anything may happen if you embrace such an unlikely stranger across the threshold of your life.

Life presents many situations that are unsettling, even abhorrent. When troubles arise, they may represent the presence of the hag, artfully disguised. There is no way to prepare for her, except to watch for her presence. She has come to test your nerve and willingness for living in a new way. Welcoming her many manifestations signals a ready and awakened consciousness. Having crossed the threshold of danger, many things—anything!—is possible.

~ 6 ~

The Morrigán, the Raven Goddess

CHAOS

Invoking the Quality of Rapid Change

The Morrigán presides at thresholds of change, namely conflict, life and death, and sexuality. On the eve of the battle, in the twilight between the armies, the Morrigán hails the victor in the shape of a great crow or raven, screaming encouragement to the favored and death to foes. Voraciously sexual, her couplings with gods and heroes render protection and fertility to the land. Her presence signifies confusion, destruction, and, especially, rapid change.

After the Tuatha Dé Danann had defeated the Fomorians, a demon-like race inhabiting Ireland, and cleared away the slaughter, the Morrigán or Mórrígu (meaning the "Terrifying" or "Great Queen") proclaimed news of victory and peace to Ireland. Joined in a single voice, the ancestors, the rivers, the summits, and the sources of waters of Ireland demanded, "What is the news?"

Peace up to heaven.
Heaven down to earth.
Earth beneath heaven,
Strength in each,
A cup very full,
Full of honey;
Mead in abundance.
Summer in winter . . .
Peace up to heaven . . .[19]

Later in mythic history, in the Ulster Cycle and the *Táin Bó Cuailnge* (The Cattle Raid of Cooley) chronicling the great conflict between the provinces of Ulster and Connacht, the war goddesses Neamhain, Badhbh, and the Morrigán terrify the Connachtmen and "a hundred warriors died of fright."[20] Appearing as a great crow or raven (see Oracle 19), the Morrigán prophesies victory to the forces of Ulster and hides the deadly news from the forces of Connacht. The great hero of the conflict is Cú Chulainn, the Hound of Ulster. Throughout the epic cycle, Cú Chulainn himself is hounded by the seductive and clever Morrigán, who both aids and ultimately defeats him. She attempts to seduce him, he spurns her, and she attacks him in revenge. She tricks him into breaking his *geis*, his sacred oath: Cú Chulainn eats the flesh of a dog, his namesake. Weakened, he goes into battle. Shortly thereafter, the Morrigán appears to him as the Washer at the Ford, washing blood from his tunic, a sure sign of approaching death:

She was washing blood-stained clothes in the stream, moaning and sobbing all the time. As Cú Chulainn watched, she lifted the garment she was washing out of the water and he saw his own tunic in her hands. Blood poured from it into the stream and turned the water red.[21]

IF YOU ARE DRAWN TO THIS ORACLE, you are approaching or are in the midst of rapid change. While the appearance of a goddess of war may appear sinister, she also clears the way for a new order once the chaos and confusion have passed. With greater spiritual maturity and experience, the presence of the Morrigán is welcomed. Following in her wake, you can quickly and even graciously rid yourself of attachments to material possessions, bankrupt relationships, and harmful or futile circumstances. This oracle is auspicious: great psychological and spiritual progress is possible. Success depends on your conscious participation, as the changes now in progress are inevitable and you cannot change them. However, by consciously observing and welcoming the changes, a new order will quickly appear, integrating remnants of your old life with new elements you never dreamed possible.

Casting this oracle may also signal the need to remain in a state of upheaval and bewilderment for a while longer. At present, no future direction can be clearly indicated, and the oracle cautions you to wait and ask again later.

~ 7 ~

Brigit, the Snake and Fire Goddess

TRANSFORMATION

Invoking the Qualities of

Imagination, Intuition, and Vision

Aligned with snakes and with fire, Brigit is the guardian of transformation and change. Present in moments of creativity and vision, she presides as midwife, prophetess, and patron of the arts, especially of poetry, hospitality, healing, breast-feeding, and the brewing of beer. The young and beautiful Brigit is composed, vigorous, passionate—and usually a virgin. Her presence inspires creativity and the capacity to meet old circumstances with renewed vision.

The Goddess Brigit, who also appears in Christianity as St. Brigit, figures powerfully in the Celtic world. In many ways, Brigit is a youthful composite of all the attributes and symbols of the Celtic goddesses in Oracles 1–4. Derived from the Gaelic word *brig*, the name Brigit means "High and Exalted One." Often appearing as three sisters, she is identified with the transforming power of the Dark Goddess herself.

Brigit's special symbols are snakes, fire, and sometimes the cow (Oracle 10). Surrounded by snakes, Brigit remains close to the earth, lending authority to transformation and change. As a child is about to be born, the attending women intone softly to invoke her presence and assistance. In Christian legend, she is known as the midwife to Mary when she gave birth to Jesus. Aligned with the element of fire to forge and mold, Brigit also presides over the hearth of the blacksmith and over imagination, vision, and prophecy. This excerpt from a simple prayer from the Scottish Highlands invokes her to shield men and women from danger at night, inspire song, and give guidance:

I am under the shielding
Of good Brigit each day;
I am under the shielding
Of good Brigit each night.

I am under the keeping
Of the Nurse of Mary,
Each early and late,
Every dark, every light.

Brigit is my comrade-woman,
Brigit is my maker of song,
Brigit is my helping-woman,
My choicest of women, my woman of guidance.[22]

The first of February (or the thirteenth of February by the old style) is the Feast of the Bride—Brigit—celebrating the coming of spring.

Brigit, as a serpent, emerges from the brown hills and turns winter to spring. Fragments of the ancient songs still survive:

The serpent will come from the hole
On the brown Day of Bride,
Though there should be three feet of snow
On the flat surface of the ground.[23]

IF YOU ARE DRAWN TO THIS ORACLE, you are attracting change and regeneration into your life. The snake goddess brings creativity and power. Domestic activities, family and friends, and circumstances close to daily activities are likely to be sources of breakthrough and insight. Old and fossilized circumstances and relationships may begin to breathe with new life, vision, and activity. Creative projects, artistic pursuits, and unexpected insights may appear in ordinary circumstances. New and creative ideas may present themselves while conversing with friends and family or while engaged in everyday activities. Now is a good time to watch for newness and allow your imagination to roam freely.

Snakes shed their dry old skin only to grow new skin. Close to the Otherworld and its powers, Brigit's snakes signify creativity as well as caution. The presence of regeneration can transform positively or can manipulate others and circumstances for personal gain. The otherworldly powers of the snake not only inspire but may also confuse, resulting in mistaking your own desires for the needs of others and even turning into trickery and deceit what may have appeared to be a worthy pursuit. Check your intuitions with the counsel of those you trust to tell you the truth.

By remaining open-hearted and generous to all, you will experience renewed vitality in everyday encounters and activities as you attract the qualities of imagination, intuition, and vision into your life.

~ 8 ~

EPONA, THE HORSE GODDESS

SAFE PASSAGE

Invoking the Qualities of Guidance and Safety

Epona the Horse Goddess brings the virility and power of the horse to the birth-giving and otherworldly powers of the mother goddesses. As the designated guardian of the dead and those in danger, she transports the dead across ocean chasms and opens the entrance to the Otherworld. Her presence lends companionship and safety during times of danger, insecurity, and challenges to health and well-being. Equally at ease on land, at sea, and in the Otherworld, Epona's guardianship is honored by the living and the dead.

Epona is always accompanied by a horse, often several horses, or foals suckling from her nipples. Appearing as a woman splendidly arrayed and riding sidesaddle on a mare, or as having the head of a woman and the body of a horse, Epona reigned as guardian of the beginnings and ends of life on earth and as local sovereign. In the Celtic world, she was revered throughout central Europe, extending in influence east to Bulgaria and west to Britain. Identified with local sovereignty to lend protection and associated with the power of horses, she was worshiped by Celts and Romans alike—especially by occupying Roman soldiers and cavalry, perhaps wanting to make some sort of propitiation to the powers of the local goddess.[24]

Aside from the mare, Epona's most distinctive imagery associates her with guarding and leading the dead to the Otherworld. Most distinctive, she carries keys, sometimes only the keys to the stables, but more likely keys to the entrance of the Otherworld.[25]

Common in mythological history, Epona is known as Macha in Ireland and Rhiannon in Wales. In the Irish *Táin Bó Cuailnge* (The Cattle Raid of Cooley) she is forced by the king to race against the king's horses. She wins, giving birth to twins as she dies at the finish, cursing the Ulster men for nine generations as her divine salvo for their cruelty. In the First Branch of the Welsh *Mabinogion*, Pwyll, Lord of Dyfed, sees Rhiannon's otherworldly horse and appearance in their first encounter. As the horsewoman approaches, Pwyll sees

> *a woman dressed in shining gold brocade and riding a great pale horse. . . . And anyone who saw the horse would have said it was moving at a slow steady pace. . . . Pwyll climbed into the saddle, but no sooner had he done so than the lady rode past him. Giving his spirited prancing mount its head he turned to follow, supposing he would overtake her at the second or third bound; yet he drew no closer than before. . . . Pwyll then called*

out, "Lady, for the sake of the man you love best, stop for me!" "I will, gladly," said she, "and it would have been better for your horse had you asked me that earlier."[26]

IF YOU ARE DRAWN TO THIS ORACLE, you are bringing protection and guidance into the current circumstances of your life. Epona can help to bring comfort to frayed nerves, companionship in dangerous or stressful situations, stamina and patience to endure and go the extra mile, and guidance in the otherworldly aspects of your passage. Her protection supports safe passage to the other side of the journey.

Epona is always seen in the company of her mare. During transition and change, you are urged to seek out the company of friends and others you trust and avoid the company of malevolent speakers or naysayers. Amid transition, you are unusually sensitive to others—even if you are not consciously aware of it, you can absorb their negative feelings and thoughts. On the other hand, sensitive times are excellent times to listen to the counsel and cautions of others, if they come from a generous heart. Trust your inner knowing to guide you amid choices, but avoid overtaxing yourself by taking in the thoughts of those you don't trust anyway. Be vigilant about the company you keep and you will receive the right guidance and kindly support.

Epona's authority to guide the otherworldly aspects of transition can assist you to stay connected to the spirit at work in your life, especially during times of great change and opportunity. Ask for guidance. Watch for shifting feelings, yearnings, or perceptions, notably things that seem especially alive or dead to you now. Look for emerging patterns seeking to be woven into your life. Trust that transitions can be times of great opportunity.

~ 9 ~

BEAR

FIERCE FEMININITY

Invoking the Quality of Selfless Actions

The wild bear of the forest is intimately linked with the Celtic goddess Artio, her very name meaning bear. Artio, the bear goddess to the Gaulish Celts, appears fiercely protective in the manner of a mother bear defending her young. She guards the bears from danger and guards humans from the bears. Accordingly, Artio personifies divine watchfulness and protection for both the human and animal realms. In human affairs, her motherly and bearlike protection brings a sense of safety, ease, and well-being.

Artio was the bear goddess of the Celts of Switzerland and the Moselle Valley during the Roman-Celtic period. While retaining the calm and tranquil bearing of the mother goddess and characteristically bearing fruit for her supplicants, Artio was nonetheless a fierce protectress. She had something of a double identity, as she was both the guardian of the bears and wild creatures of the forest, and the guardian of the sacred hunt.[27]

Like a mother bear defending her young, Artio watched over animals and humans alike. Fiercely loyal, she was venerated by the Celts for the protection she provided against the wild forces of nature and, by extension, against enemies. Hunters and warriors propitiated her interventions. When enraged she was aggressive and dominant. Raging like a mother bear protecting her young in times of danger, the Celts felt safer under her sway.

Artio's fierce qualities resemble the "Mother Terrible" aspect of the goddesses of Old Europe from the Balkans discussed by Marija Gimbatas (6500–3500 B.C.).[28] Artio's supernatural character may be a remnant from a time when goddesses were revered as the primal forces of nature, presiding over life, regeneration, and death. While Celtic mythology abounds in stories of fiery goddesses and queens, archaeological evidence for Artio (or other ferociously dominant goddesses) is scarce. A small bronze statue found near Berne, Switzerland, depicts a regal Artio bearing fruit before the full figure of a bear,[29] who appears to be greeting her. Between them is intimate identification, as though they are matched in strength and ferocity and equally divine.

IF YOU ARE DRAWN TO THIS ORACLE, this may be an ideal time to develop the fierce, feminine qualities of readiness and responsibility for others into your character. Not only does the mother bear protect her own young, but she personifies selfless, courageous acts on behalf of others. She acts immediately and powerfully in service to others to protect and preserve in times of danger and distress. Her actions bring peace and tranquillity to life. Everyone benefits from her watchful attention and protection.

Being watchful and safeguarding the rightful needs of family, kin, and community are beneficial and necessary qualities in human life. Men and women are called on to intervene and mediate when the rights of others are unjustly violated or circumscribed. Trust your immediate and selfless response to situations when others are in need or danger. There is no reason to hold back and think about it. Act.

~ 10 ~

Cow

INEXHAUSTIBLE SUPPLY

Invoking an Open and Generous Heart

Sacred to the goddess, the cow is a legendary source of wealth and nurturance. Symbolizing sovereignty and title, Celtic goddesses and queens guard their cattle jealously. As a newborn, the goddess Brigit is washed in milk and nurtured on the milk of an otherworldly cow. Folk legends from Ireland and Wales describe wondrous cows whose inexhaustible supply of milk never runs dry and faery cows who calve every year and give plentiful milk to the poor. The cow of the goddess represents generosity of spirit.

The oldest tales of Ireland tell of otherworldly cows whose inexhaustible supply of milk is the envy of their neighbors. Long ago, a people with great powers known as the "People of the Goddess," the Tuatha Dé Danaan, lived in Ireland. Among their enemies were the Fomorians, a demonlike race who had fled Ireland to live on islands in the north. The Fomorian king has an evil eye: with one glance his enemies drop dead. Though he has plenty of cattle, he envies a wondrous cow, the Glas Gaibhleann, whose milk never runs dry and is guarded night and day by her owner, a man of the Tuatha Dé called Cian. One day Balor sees his chance to seize the cow. Turning himself into a redheaded boy, Balor tricks Cian into deserting the cow for an instant. Balor regains his own nature, seizes the cow, and drags her behind him by the tail, crossing the sea to the safety of his own island. The myth continues, for now it is Cian's turn to steal the wondrous cow.

In early times, families were eager to have a ready supply of milk to sustain the life of the family and especially the newborns. The hope for a constant supply of milk was invested in the goddesses, and especially with Brigit (Oracle 7). The Festival of Brigit on February 1, coinciding with the arrival of newborn calves and lambs, celebrates the end of the scarcity of winter and arrival of the new milk of spring. In January, when milk was scarce, the old people used to say that it wouldn't be long now till Brigit and her white cow would be coming.[30] Cows and their newborn calves were put under Brigit's protection:

> *The new springer was always put under St. Brigit's protection. After she calved and before being let out on grass a sort of ceremony was performed by the man and woman of the house. One stood each side of the cow and then passed a tongs of coals round over her kidneys and under her udder three times, and repeating prayers to St. Brigit as they did so. When the coals were quenched by throwing them in the drain in the cowhouse and a red rag containing a cinder and a grain of salt was tied*

on the tail, a drop of holy water was sprinkled on the cow and she was driven with great ceremony to join the herd. The spancel [farm tool] and the tongs were flung after her and then picked up and put away. How the tongs fell foretold how lucky the milker would be, and being touched with her old spancel protected her from fairies or spells of any kind.[31]

In Irish folk tradition, Brigit's cow is sometimes identified with the famous cow of famine times whose supply of milk is inexhaustible and runs into a sieve until the cow runs dry. A Welsh story tells the same sad tale: On a fine day, a parti-colored cow—perhaps a faery cow—appears on the moorlands of Denbighshire, and everyone in need goes to her for a rich supply of milk, and her milk never runs dry. Finally, a wicked woman milks her into a riddle (coarse sieve) until she runs dry. At once, the cow, bellowing miserably, disappears under the waters of a nearby lake.[32]

IF YOU ARE DRAWN TO THIS ORACLE, you are yearning to welcome opportunities to both give and receive nurturance, compassion, and hospitality. Great goodness and satisfaction can be found in giving and receiving of nurturance. Especially important is the sharing of good food, hospitality, great coffee, laughter, and friendship in the lively and convivial company of friends, colleagues, and family. Depending on the circumstances, you may be the recipient of unexpected caring and attention from others. Under different conditions, you may want to share with friends or give hospitality to strangers. Welcome the stranger, the outsider, and the disenfranchised. Draw close to the concerns that pull at your heart in a personal way. By cultivating a ready attitude of giving, receiving becomes easier, and more natural, too.

Symbolic of the abundance of the goddesses, the cow's supply of milk is unbounded. Forethought and discretion are wise, but anxious planning for the future brings heartache and strain. It is possible to live more in the present moment, trusting that what you need will come to you. The cow signals that the inexhaustible supply of life surrounds you.

~ II ~

Lap Dog, Hound of the Goddess

INTIMACY WITH SELF

Invoking the Quality of Loving Attention

The hound of the goddess conveys gentle companionship to the innermost promptings of the human spirit. Unlike the harrowing hound of hell in Mediterranean mythology, the Celtic hound is kind and helpful, usually sitting at the goddess's feet, resting in her lap, gazing adoringly, or even nursing from her breasts. Associated with the regenerative powers of the Otherworld, the lap dog brings healing and loving attention to our deep emotional and spiritual natures.

A magical encounter with otherworldly hounds is found in the First Branch of the Welsh *Mabinogion*, when Pwyll, Lord of Dyfed, is out hunting with his own pack of hounds:

> *As he listened to the baying of his pack [of hounds] he perceived the cry of another pack, a different cry which was advancing towards him. He spied a clearing in the forest, a level field, and as his pack reached the edge of this field he saw the other pack with a stag running before it, and near the centre of the clearing this other pack overtook the stag and brought it down. Pwyll at once remarked on the pack's colour, without bothering to look at the stag, for no hound he had ever seen was the colour of these: a dazzling shining white with red ears, and as the whiteness of the dogs shone so did the redness of their ears.*[33]

The hounds of the goddess epitomize the domestic dog at its best—affectionate, watchful, attentive, and loyal. Allied with the healing powers of the Otherworld, the hounds convey the gentle and regenerative powers of the spirit world to heal and restore. Throughout the Celtic world, like the goddess herself, hounds are symbols of nourishment and sustenance, and especially of companionship, even accompanying the goddess in the sacred hunt.[34] The popular Celtic goddess of the North Sea, Nehalennia, was especially favored by seafarers who invoked her protection on their hazardous crossings. Nehalennia is never without her constant companions, an otherworldly hound or two, sitting on her lap and heedful of her wishes.[35]

Ever vigilant and faithful, the hounds bring the reassurance of divine favor and trustworthy intimacy with the healing and restorative powers of the spirit world.

IF YOU ARE DRAWN TO THIS ORACLE, you are attracting the benevolent forces of the spirit world to transform your life from within. It is a graced and auspicious time to heal and strengthen the inmost self. Old, deep wounds may be soothed and resolved without trauma or even conscious attention. Harmful patterns and habits may dissolve effortlessly. Troublesome relationships may clear up, slip away easily, or clear up in healthier and more beneficial ways.

You have only to let the changes occur naturally. You are asked to trust, allowing changes to unfold freely. The natural cycle of death and regeneration are working quietly on your behalf. Try not to interfere through overactivity, thinking too much, wallowing in your troubles or insecurities, or planning the rest of your life. Taking time to meditate and not hurrying may give more spaciousness to the process of change.

Drawing this oracle suggests that the spirit world is now working in a very personal way to assist you. It is as if you are getting a little extra attention right now. Positive changes are already moving within you.

~ 12 ~

Mare

HEALING THE WOUNDS OF ABANDONMENT, BETRAYAL, AND LOSS OF TRUST

Invoking the Qualities of Confidence and Hope

The mare brings strength and beauty into human activities. As an animal of great nobility, she carries the human spirit through its darkest hours. As the Great High Queen, Rhiannon, she is betrayed by her attendants, husband, and subjects, who blame her for killing her newborn son. When her son is eventually returned, Rhiannon names him Pryderi, meaning "for my troubles." The mare signifies the return to wholeness and the renewal of hope.

The most startling image of a Celtic horse is the enormous White Horse of Uffington, cut into the hillside above Uffington in Wessex, England. Placed high on the hill and packed with layers of chalk, the white horse overlooks the wide, green countryside. Like the horse images on Celtic coins, her Iron Age image is stylized, rather than naturalistic, and her nose is curiously beaked like a bird.[36]

In the First Branch of the Welsh *Mabinogion*, Rhiannon is both queen and mare. Her marriage to Pwyll, Lord of Dyfed, is celebrated with great feasting, merriment, and the giving of gifts. Rhiannon becomes known as a bountiful queen for her generous gifts. Yet, after several years of anticipation, when Rhiannon gives birth to a son, she is perilously betrayed:

> *On the night of his birth women were brought in to look after mother and child, but these women and Rhiannon all fell asleep. Six women had been brought into the chamber, and they did watch for part of the night, but they were asleep before midnight and woke only at dawn; upon waking they searched round where they had left the boy, but there wasn't a trace of him. "Alas! The boy is lost!" said one woman. "Yes," said another, "and they would consider it getting off lightly if we were only burned and executed." "Is there any hope for us?" "There is—I have a good plan." "What is it?" they all asked. "There is a deerhound here with pups. We can kill some of the pups, smear Rhiannon's hands and face with the blood, throw the bones before her and insist that she destroyed her own child—it will be her word against that of us six.*[37]

In punishment for killing her son, Rhiannon must wait at the horse mount and offer to carry guests and strangers to the palace on her back. Most refuse the mare's offer. Even in her punishment and betrayal, her unqualified beauty heralds dignity and strength. Like the mares associated with Epona, the Horse Goddess, Rhiannon as an otherworldly mare passes safely through danger—and in Rhiannon's case, through loss, betrayal, and indignity.

IF YOU ARE DRAWN TO THIS ORACLE, you are seeking to heal old hurts, anxieties, or traumas. Abandonment, betrayal, and the consequent loss of trust leave the heart wounded, fearful, and closed. In drawing this oracle, your heart seeks to be more open and free. The mare's enduring strength and stamina will support you through pain and discomfort into renewed awareness, reconciliation, and understanding.

In the days ahead, you may be challenged by new insights into old situations. Old patterns may replay themselves in new guises. Memories of the past may reemerge and seem abhorrent to you. Consider meeting these challenges as opportunities to grow and heal. With the extra courage and stamina available to you now, it will be easier to revisit old circumstances than in the past. Though insights will occur, do not expect extraordinary insights every day. Over time, confidence, hope, and trust in the future will be restored. Power will return to you.

~ 13 ~
Coupling of Earth and Sky

Unlimited Possibilities

Invoking the Qualities of Patience and Steadiness

The mythical sexual union of the sovereign goddess with a god or mortal king conveys fertility and prosperity to the land. Throughout Welsh and Irish legend, the sexual union of the sovereign goddess and a mortal man elects the man as king and grants him otherworldly powers, so long as he is just. The goddess Morrigán mates with Daghdha, the great tribal god. The queen-goddess Medb (meaning "one who intoxicates") chose and tested her many sexual partners. The coupling of earth and sky signifies unlimited possibilities.

The sexual coupling between the sovereign goddess with a tribal god or mortal king signifies the bringing of otherworldly blessing to people, animals, and crops. The goddess signifies the spirit of the land itself, the man its protector. The royal court at Tara, the mythological heart of Ireland, was traditionally the site of the ritual enactment of union between the king and the land, represented by the goddess of sovereignty. The mythic exchange of sexual potency assured new offspring and vigor, and brought fluorescence to plants and flowers. The people and animals were fertile. The sun shone and rains came to nourish the fields. The harvests were regular and abundant. The people grew healthy, prosperous, and joyous.

One of the many manifestations of the sovereign goddess is the Morrigán (of Oracle 6), often associated with protecting the land in times of war. The Morrigán is a great warrior, fierce in battle, but here is associated with fertility, courage, and bold sexuality. The *Dindshenchas*, a twelfth-century manuscript linking topography and myth, describes her role as sovereign of fecundity. The Morrigán mates with the Daghdha, the tribal god, as she stands straddling a river, with one of her two feet on the south of the water and the other to the north of the water. In a place known as the Bed of the Couple, they have sexual intercourse, thereby assuring the fertility of the people and animals and fruitfulness of the land.

The earlier the legend, the more prominent is the goddess's role in electing the future king of Ireland. The queen-goddess Medb's intrepid sexuality was but her duty in choosing the best consort possible for the well-being and protection of Ireland. Often manifesting as the hag of Oracle 5, the sovereign goddess elects the king independently, choosing the best candidate from among the royal line. The coupling takes place once one has passed the hag's terrifying tests.

Without union with the sovereign goddess, the spirit of the land, no king can rule justly and wisely. The sexual union of the goddess with a mortal man elects him as king. As long as he is just, she grants him otherworldly powers and the land flourishes with bounty.

IF YOU ARE DRAWN TO THIS ORACLE, anticipate the unexpected. The essence of the earth and sky, represented by the union of the sovereign goddess and mortal man, are joining to prepare a common accord and showing of blessing.

The new is possible, yet the success of this transition depends on your attitude. Sexual union creates urgency and possibility. The intensity of sexual coupling, the union of opposites, and the exchange of energy signify the heat of transformation and life. While the "marriage" of these forces is already within you, the force of birth requires patience and steadiness. New life is precious and requires grand attention and care. Be patient and steady. You may even have to slow down and pace yourself, as sexual energy discharged erratically can cause unnecessary confusion. Allow your life to be spacious and comfortable, so that new life and new possibilities have a chance to grow and develop easily. Nothing can be hurried. If you are receptive and steady, new possibilities will take root within you. If growth is even and unhurried, the possibilities are great.

~ 14 ~

Sacred King

THE OATH

Invoking the Qualities of Honor and Responsibility

If the royal cloak fits him, the royal chariot obeys him, the Stone of Fál at Tara shrieks at his touch, and the goddess joins with him, a mortal man will be chosen king of Ireland. Bound by sacred oaths, *geissi,* to govern wisely and protect his people, the king's authority is carefully constrained and obliged by duty. The destiny of the king and his reign and the land and its bounty depend on the king's fealty to the royal oaths. The sacred king signifies honorable and responsible actions.

In former times, before the Norman conquest of Britain and coastal Ireland and Wales, Celtic kings were chosen by the sovereign goddess who granted the new king otherworldly powers so as to reign justly and wisely. To find the rightful man among the young men of the royal clan, the candidates were watched and tested by the druids for signs of providence. Niall of the Nine Hostages was born by a well, a sacred threshold to the Otherworld. Later, he meets and couples with the goddess there and is elected king of Ireland.

The tests of honor for the rightful king remain much the same throughout history. The king must show exceptional virtue, as though already appointed by the Otherworld. In Ireland, according to tradition, the royal cloak must fit him, the royal chariot must obey him, and the Stone of Fál at Tara must shriek when he touches it. Then, the sovereign goddess of the land must accept him as her own choice from among the others. In myth, their union is sexual: the exchange of primal energies bringing fertility and greenery to the land. Recorded in the twelfth century by the Roman chronicler Giraldus Cambrensis (Gerald of Wales) was the ritual bath of the Ulster king in the broth that boiled the butchered flesh of a white mare, symbolizing the sovereign goddess.[38] At the royal court at Tara, the heart of legendary Ireland, their union is ritually reenacted. Ériu, a goddess and namesake of Ireland, offers a gold goblet of red wine to successive kings, symbolizing their union and her promise through this union to bless the land with ceaseless bounty.[39]

Once elected, the king is bound by sacred oaths and strict rules of conduct, securing that his reign will provide for the well-being, prosperity, and protection of the people. He is not free to do as he pleases and follow his whims. He is bound by rules of fealty and honor, the betrayal of which signals his individual ruin, a lackluster reign, the failure of crops, and the demoralization of his people. His only honorable choice, once king, is to govern wisely and justly, speak only the truth and keep his promises, show impartiality, provide protection to the weak and the strong alike, render hospitality, take up arms to defend the people from enemies, and in his noble conduct set a standard for all to follow.

IF YOU ARE DRAWN TO THIS ORACLE, your actions must be especially honorable and unselfish. You are in a situation of responsibility asking you to protect the well-being of others. Your sense of honor and duty demand that you put aside personal inclinations to serve others.

In order to be successful, your actions must be honest and impartial. In the present situation, your personal likes and dislikes, or impressions formed in the past, may be untrustworthy. Make decisions based on what is valid and invalid, on the weaknesses and strengths inherent in the specific circumstance. Tell the truth and keep your promises. Accept responsibility graciously. Extend generosity and concern, especially to those who are less fortunate in your community. Be mindful that your personal life is now an aspect of your public life and that your actions set an example for others.

~ 15 ~

Divine Couple

UNION

Invoking the Qualities of Harmony and Balance

The divine couple represents the auspicious union of the goddess of the land and the god of fertility. As lovers, their constant and faithful alliance provide harmony and prosperity to households and settlements. Equal in stature and supernatural powers, the paired deities personify the balanced ordering of life and confidence in life's continuance, even after death. Their pairing signifies health and abundance in the seamless passage of time and events.

Divine couples are a common feature of Celtic iconography, even more so than among the Greeks and Romans. Popular local goddesses personifying the land partner with gods of fertility and prosperity to assure the continuance of life.

In areas occupied by Roman armies, native goddesses acquired Roman gods as partners, creatively sanctioning both a military and a spiritual reality. Portrayed as equal in size and balanced in authority, these divine partners provided assurance of the orderly continuance of life through the dangers and unpredictability of daily life amid conquest and occupation, and even beyond the portals of death.

Together as partners, or individually, Sucellus the Hammer God (Oracle 55), and Nantosuelta, a territorial river goddess, were widely revered throughout Provence, Burgundy, Germany, and Luxembourg. They are a handsome couple of equal size and proportions, usually portrayed seated beside each other on thrones or standing regally, accompanied by their individual symbols of authority. He holds a hammer or mallet, and sometimes a pot; she carries a cornucopia or plate of fruits and grains, and occasionally a scepter festooned with a symbol of a house. Together they are associated with prosperity, health, and well-being, the success of the wine harvest, and through regeneration the protection of the living and the dead.[40]

In occupied areas of Gaul, Germany, and Britain, Mercury and Apollo became popular among the Celts, Apollo even acquiring several Celtic surnames. Though Mercury retains his winged cap and Apollo his lyre, they are nonetheless paired with the native Celtic goddesses, Rosmerta and Sirona respectively. One of Rosmerta's characteristics includes holding a rudder perched on a globe, as though to guide it. Sirona is associated with curative thermal springs and healing. Though divine couples were usually portrayed as equals, a unique stone from the Rhineland in Germany suggests Rosmerta's authority over the Roman Mercury. The iconography shows the Roman god offering his money bag to Rosmerta, who sits before him on a throne.[41]

Irish and Welsh legends are full of the intrigues of supernatural lovers, often the background or rationale for war. There is no way to directly compare these figures with the divine couples of Roman-Celtic iconography, except to point out a common lineage. Like the supernatural couples of an earlier time, the female heroines are active and forthright, and scarcely the pawns of male intrigue. Indeed, like evenly matched teams, their equal powers animate the action.

IF YOU ARE DRAWN TO THIS ORACLE, you are seeking to bring confidence and strength into your life through the balancing of powers. No real success—in the external affairs of life or in the inner life—is achieved through domination or force. In time, those things achieved by force will always feel shallow and unsatisfying.

Having drawn this oracle, you are attracting to your life a situation asking you to balance strength with compassion and action with tenderness. You may wish to examine and explore aspects of your life that could be brought into greater balance. The feminine and masculine powers within you are seeking to become strong and resilient so that true balance may permeate all of your life. The harmony gained in the balancing of opposites will bring confidence and success to your personal and professional life and assurance in the continuity of life amid external changes.

~ 16 ~

Wondrous Child

PROMISE

Invoking the Qualities of Hope and Trust in the Future

The Wondrous Child conveys promise and the rekindling of hope and trust in the future. In Irish legend, the wondrous child is Cú Chulainn. As a boy of seven, he was already the greatest combatant in the court of the king, Conor Mac Nessa, and he grows up to defend all of Ulster single-handedly. Taliesin, the great bard of Wales, is another wondrous child. When as a child he is discovered in a leather bag in a salmon weir, he composes poetry recounting the feats of his fabulous origins.

Throughout the world, the birth of exceptional children is a sign of hope. In Celtic lore and legend, the origins and childhood of great poets, saints, musicians, and warriors are often miraculous in character. Cú Chulainn, the great hero of the Ulster Cycle, was the son of none other than the god Lugh of the Long Arm (Oracle 60) of the Tuatha Dé Danann and Dechtire, sister of the King of Ulster, Conor Mac Nessa. Oengus, the youthful champion of Oracle 59, was the son of the river goddess Bóinn and Daghdha, the Good God.

Taliesin (Oracle 51), the incomparable bard of Wales, had once been a boy called Gwion Bach. Upon "accidentally" acquiring knowledge of all there was to know, he incurs the wrath of Ceridwen the Hag, who chases him as a greyhound when he is a hare, as an otter when he is a fish, and as a hawk when he is a bird. Finally, as a hen, she eats him when he is a grain of winnowed wheat on the floor of a barn. The grain of wheat passes into her womb, and in nine months she gives birth to a son so fair and beautiful that she cannot bear to slay him. So she puts him in a leather bag and watches him while he shape-shifts into a hare, a fish, a bird, and finally into a grain of wheat. Immediately, Ceridwen eats him and the seed goes into her womb. Nine months later, Taliesin is born once again as a boy so fair and beautiful that Ceridwen, unable to kill him, places him in a leather bag (in some versions a basket) and sets him to drift on a river on the eve of Beltaine.

Meanwhile, the son of a nobleman, called Elffin, known for his terribly bad luck, is sent by his father to a favored salmon weir. Every May Eve, the father was accustomed to taking salmon of great value from the weir, but Elffin finds nothing but a plain leather bag. When Elffin slices the bag open, he sees a bright forehead, and cries, "Look, a radiant brow (*tal iesin*)." Elffin is despondent over the bad luck of returning to his father's court with nothing but a child. But the boy astride Elffin's saddle begins at once to compose a poem for him. Amazed, Elffin asks him how he could possibly compose such poetry, being so young. Taliesin replies with another poem, known as "The Consolation of Elffin":

Elffin of noble generosity,
Do not sorrow at your catch.
Though I am weak on the floor of my basket,
There are wonders on my tongue.
While I am watching over you,
No great need will overcome you . . .[42]

IF YOU ARE DRAWN TO THIS ORACLE, you are urged to cherish and develop a talent or skill that is latent within yourself or in someone you love. It may be a child, a friend, a partner, or even a teacher. Whether you need to attend to yourself or someone else, the talent in question is extraordinary in some unique way. If the talent is within you, you will need to create an environment that allows for long stretches of unencumbered time to practice or cultivate the essential skills. Garnering unencumbered time in modern life may require major reordering of priorities. If you are in the role of supporting another, you are in the role of an assistant and supporter who makes time and more supportive environments possible. Either way, you are a great encourager of self or another. New life in all forms is invariably innocent, potential, and incomplete. The role of encouraging, supporting, and providing safety are essential to its secure development.

Part Two

Oracles of Nature's Wisdoms

Those oracles relating to:

Animals

Sovereignty in the Animal Realm

Ancient Trees and Scepters

Elemental Spirits

~ 17 ~

Boar

FEARLESS IN CONFLICT

Invoking Strong and Decisive Actions

The wild boar is revered for its ferocity and strength. By association, weapons and armor adorned with boar symbols lend fury and courage to warriors. Arduinna, a boar goddess and huntress from the Ardennes Forest in northern Gaul, rides bareback on a galloping boar. Arawn, the Lord of the Welsh Otherworld, rewards Pwyll for his bravery with the precious gift of the first herd of pigs in Wales. The wild boar signifies power, strength, and fearlessness in conflict.

Wild boars personify the terror of war. Celtic weapons and armor bear the symbols of the boar, its mouth menacingly open and dorsal bristles standing straight up. Replete with screaming, yelling, clamoring chariots, clashing weapons, and the neighing of terrified horses, Celtic battles were horrifying, bloody, and noisy. Roaring over the hill in wild abandon and screeching savagely, enemies were often reduced to terror by the tumult. Adding to the din, among the horns are trumpets called carnyxes, fashioned in the shape of a boar's head, its mouth open and snarling. When blown, carnyxes add a horrid, rattling screech to the fury of battle.[43]

Boars and pigs are also prized for their meat. They demand great skill and courage from the hunters and their horses in the hunt. Though often exaggerated, the Celtic fondness for pork and ritual feasting is well known and documented. Warriors extolling their bravery competed for the champion's portion of pork at the feast. Choice pieces of pork were buried with chieftains to prepare them for otherworldly feasting. Pig offerings were made to the gods, sometimes slaughtered with select portions buried as gifts to the Otherworld, butchered and given as food offerings, or consumed in ritual feasting.[44]

The legends from Wales and Ireland portray boars as supernatural, enchanted, and as gifts from the Otherworld. In the First Branch of the Welsh *Mabinogion*, Pwyll, Lord of Llys Aberth, encounters Arawn, Lord of the Otherworld. For breaking an honor code, Pwyll must exchange places with Arawn for a year and slay his otherworldly enemy, Hafgan. Pwyll keeps his pledge, and after the year is over Pwyll and Arawn return to their own realms. In gratitude, Arawn sends Pwyll and later his son Pryderi wondrous gifts, the most precious being the first herd of pigs in Wales. In "Math the Son of Mathonwy" of the *Mabinogion*, which chronicles the conflict between northern and southern Wales, the magician Math, the Lord of Gwynedd, envies the otherworldly pigs:

So they went unto Math the Son of Mathonwy. "Lord," said Gwydion, "I have heard that there have appeared in the South some beasts such as were never known in this island before." "What are they called?" asked Math. "Pigs, lord." "And what kind of animals are they?" "They are small animals, and their flesh is better than the flesh of oxen. . . ." "And who owneth them?" "Pryderi the son of Pwyll; they were sent to him from Annwn, by Arawn the king of Annwn. . . ." "And by what means may they be obtained from him?" "I will go, lord, as one of twelve, in the guise of bards, to seek the swine." "It may be that he will refuse you," said Math. "I will not come back without the swine," replied Gwydion. "Gladly," said Math, "go thou forward."[45]

In the *Tale of Culhwch and Olwen*, Culhwch is of royal birth and cousin of Arthur. Cursed for offending a queen, Culhwch falls in love with Olwen, the daughter of the giant Ysbaddaden. Since Olwen's marriage prefigures the giant's death, Culhwch is given a series of extraordinary tasks to perform by the giant before he can win the hand of Olwen. His quest centers on capturing Twrch Trwyth, a fierce and enchanted boar who was once an evil king, and seizing the shears, comb, and razor from between Twrch Trwyth's ears. Enlisting the aid of Arthur and Mabon, son of the goddess Modron, Culhwch follows Twrch Trwyth and his band of enchanted pigs all over southern Wales, Ireland, and Cornwall before bringing Twrch Trwyth to the ground.[46]

IF YOU ARE DRAWN TO THIS ORACLE, the conditions ask for strong and decisive actions. To act with power and strength, you must first seek clarity and then act decisively. Conflict, disagreements, and discord can be multiplied by indecision and vacillation. The wild boar is never indecisive, but moves swiftly forward. While the aggression of the boar is needed in everyday life, a fierce focus and determinism are often required in business and professional life. Sometimes you must fight for what you need.

When applied to personal or intimate affairs, this oracle points to swift and decisive actions to curtail misunderstandings or even to stop the actions of others when safety or security is threatened. In specific circumstances, you must protect and defend yourself, physically and emotionally, from the actions of others. Stay centered and resolute.

~ 18 ~

Water Horses

MAGICAL ENCOUNTERS

Invoking the Union of Strength and Beauty

Water horses and sea horses appear riding across the seas or arising from the depths of lochs. Like sky horses drawing the sun's chariots across the skies in prehistoric drawings, mythic sea horses convey the chariots of the god of the seas, Manannán Mac Lir, and his entourage across oceans. In folk stories, swift and radiant water horses arise from the depths of inland lakes to bring prosperity to those who respect and provide for them. The water horse represents strength and beauty crossing into our lives.

Crossing the seas or arising from the depths of inland lochs, water horses and sea horses bring a bright union of strength and beauty. Glistening in the sun, they combine the strength and vigor of a horse, the radiance of sun in swift flight, and the mystery of its origins beneath the sea. In *The Voyage of Bran*, a mythical sea horse conveys the chariot of the god of the seas, Manannán Mac Lir, and his company to meet Bran and his sailors, who are in search of the enchanted isle. As Manannán comes closer to the boat he begins to sing:

Bran's boat skims over calm waters,
Bran's ship is reveling in a clear sea, but to me,
in my chariot, it is a flowery plain.
In my gentle land, the home of Manannán Mac Lir, sea horses
glisten in the sun, and rivers pour forth honey.
Flowers are growing where Bran sees waves. . . .

Row steadily, Bran, row steadily over my kingdom and you
will reach the Land of Women before the setting of the sun.[47]

Manannán and his chariot disappear beneath the waves and Bran and his sailors row on.

Like mythical sea horses, water horses radiate strength and beauty in popular tales from Ireland and Scotland. Many of the stories tell of a poor farmer whose farm is near a lake or the sea. One day he discovers a foal in his field and she grows into a magnificent mare. She is beautiful, of "fine limb and graceful form" and as "swift as the wind and had no equal."[48] Many years later, he mistreats her and she disappears with her foals back into the sea. In a typical story from County Sligo in Ireland, a poor farmer encounters a foal grazing on the shore near his small house:

One morning when he got up he went out to the well for a can of water for his tea. To his great surprise, he saw a young foal on the shore. He went down to the shore and brought the foal in. The foal grew to a mare and every year she had a foal. This continued for seven years and after some time he was a rich man. . . . But one morning a strange thing happened. The man went out to the stable to let out the mare. When he was letting her out, he hit her with her bridle. As soon as he did, the mare neighed seven times and the seven foals came galloping up to her. They all turned in the direction of the sea and swam out into the water. They were never seen again.[49]

IF YOU ARE DRAWN TO THIS ORACLE, you are called to renew some aspect of your life with the joining of beauty and strength. Perhaps your life now feels too familiar, routine, conforming, or emotionally flat. Your daily activities may lack spontaneity and vigor. Male or female, the depths of your masculinity may long for opportunities to explore new strengths and capacities. You may wish to express your outward authority, mastery, and leadership in tender and gracious ways. If so, new challenges and experiences may be drawing close. Your judgment and skill will be tested. Opportunities to explore the unknown may enter your life. By joining beauty to strength, you have the opportunity to break out of the overly familiar and experience vigorous and harmonious ways of living and acting.

~ 19 ~

Raven

TRUTH-TELLING AND PROPHESY

Invoking the Qualities of

Insight, Clarity, and Discrimination

The earliest depictions of the raven are found drawn on prehistoric cave walls. Large ravens are portrayed speaking to human figures, as though prophesying from the chthonic to the earthly realms. Irish druids watch the flight of ravens to predict the future. Appearing as ravens, goddesses wreak havoc among armies, predicting death and the outcomes of battles. As a messenger from the Otherworld, the raven signifies speaking the truth and prophecy.

Like mother goddesses, carrion birds are complex symbols of death and rebirth. Statuary and coins depicting carrion birds hint at myths and symbols long forgotten by history. At temple shrines dedicated to the mother goddess Nantosuelta, ravens perch near her as though bearing messages from the Otherworld.[50] Unique Celtic coins suggest an unknown story: an immense raven rides on the back of a horse. The reins appear to be held by the bird, and its talons dig deeply into the horse's back. Sometimes carrying a small cake in its beak, the raven may be bearing fruit or gifts from the Otherworld.[51]

The earliest traces of Celtic art are cave drawings found in the Camonica Valley in the Italian Alps near Brescia, the work of Iron and Bronze Age Celts. Ravens appear to speak to a human figure who stands before the bird, as though listening.[52]

Evocative of an intimate connection between the birds and goddesses is the mysterious winged goddess.[53] She appears as both in this world and of another world. While shape-shifting between forms is commonplace in Celtic images, portrayals are rarely "frozen" midway in transition. Like the raven, the winged goddess may be a messenger between the realms, bearing gifts as well as prophesies.

From the Iron and Bronze Age through the Roman period, ravens appear as benign, even auspicious, in their accustomed role as prophets and messengers from the Otherworld. However, in the warrior culture of medieval Ireland, their aspect changes. Forecasting death and carnage on the battlefield, tales of terror recount a better story. In the celebrated account in the Ulster Cycle of the death of Cú Chulainn, the Hound of Ulster, the truth-telling Morrigán (Oracle 6) appears as a raven and concludes the scene:

> ***Holding the huge wound in his body together, Cúchulainn . . . took a drink and washed himself and turned from the lake to die. On the shore, a little distance away, he saw a pillar stone and he struggled towards it and put his back to it for support.***

Then he took his belt and tied himself to the pillar so that he would die standing up, for he had sworn he would meet his end "feet on the ground, face to the foe." Upright and facing his enemies, he called to them to come near him and cautiously they approached and stood round him silently in a circle. They stayed there and watched him but none of them dared lay a hand on him for the hero light still shone round his head. . . .

For three days his enemies watched Cúchulainn. The ravens of battle, the Morrigu and Badb, hovered around his head and at last the hero light faltered, flickered, and went out. As it did so, Cúchulainn let out a great sigh and the pillar stone split at his back. A raven lit on his shoulder and settled there.[54]

IF YOU ARE DRAWN TO THIS ORACLE, the raven is your benefactor and companion. Your present situation may require speaking the truth in order to clear the way for newness and avoid misunderstandings. Regardless of the situation, lying about mundane or important aspects of your life tears at the fabric of your nature because it disables your emotional and spiritual maturity. On the other hand, bludgeoning others with your opinion without cause or necessity is not mature truth-telling, either. Telling the truth means seeing the world clearly and speaking what you see.

Telling the truth is akin to prophesy. It cleans the "eye of the heart." In time your inner vision will see things in their essence and into events seeming to take place in the future. Having been drawn to this oracle, you may have an opportunity to open the windows of perception, to see more deeply into life, and to bring insight and discrimination from the world of spirit to the ordinary, seemingly mundane affairs of life.

~ 20 ~

Salmon

KNOWLEDGE

Invoking Spontaneity and Artistry

The magical salmon brings supernatural knowledge and wisdom. Taliesin, the ancient bard of Wales, was retrieved from a salmon weir in the River Conwy. In the Finn Cycle of Ireland, the red-speckled salmon living in a pool on the River Boyne acquires great knowledge by eating the berries of the rowan tree overhanging the pool. When Finn tastes one of the salmon, he acquires knowledge of everything in the world, past, present, and future, and becomes as great a poet as he is a warrior and hunter.

In Irish and Welsh legends, the salmon captures the wonders of otherworldly wisdom. Swimming in pools close to sacred springs (see Oracle 38) and feeding on rowan berries (see Oracle 26), salmon acquire knowledge of all there is to know.

The Finn Cycle of Ireland chronicles the story of a magic salmon and the giving of the knowledge of all things to Finn. To acquire greater wisdom, Finn goes to learn poetry from Finneces, who lives on the shores of the magical River Boyne (Bóinn), encamped there for seven years attempting to catch one of the red-speckled salmon that live in a pool by the river. The salmon eat the berries that fall from a rowan tree overhanging the pool and acquire the knowledge of all there ever was to know. Whoever eats one of the salmon will enjoy the wisdom of the world. When Finn comes to Finneces's camp, the poet has just caught a beautiful salmon. Finneces gives the fish to Finn and instructs him to cook it, but not to eat even the smallest piece. While lifting the salmon off the spit, the skin of fish sears Finn's thumb. Thrusting his thumb into his mouth to ease the pain, the knowledge intended for Finneces goes to Finn. As prophesied, the wisdom of the salmon goes to a fair-haired man named Finn who becomes as great "a poet as he was a warrior and hunter."[55]

If you are drawn to this oracle, the unspoiled wisdoms within your nature seek expression in the creative arts, especially poetry, prose, drama, and singing. Even without special training or talent, creative pursuits seem satisfying and want to be spontaneously expressed. Routine activities may suddenly seem revitalized with insight. Creative and ingenious people attract you. The grandeur of nature is a great source of joy and inspiration.

In the Celtic world, the bards could both bless and curse with the eloquence of their words. In our time, words can promote good and evil and, therefore, rightful expression requires clarity of mind and heart. Take time to choose your words and expressions carefully.

Like the magical salmon feeding on the rowan berries at the bottom of the pool, wisdom may seem to come from a deep well within you. Fresh insights may nourish many aspects of your life, personally and professionally. New ideas will beg expression in words. If you respect the rights of others, this new (or renewed) artistry in ideas and words will develop and increase.

~ 21 ~

Cernunnos, Antlered God

Lord of the Animals

Invoking the Qualities of Generosity and Magnanimity

As Lord of the Animals, Cernunnos provides refuge, sustenance, and well-being for the animals of the great forests of Europe. Majestically portrayed on the Gundestrup Cauldron, the antlered Cernunnos sits cross-legged on the ground next to a great stag. Cernunnos also appears intimately allied with the mother goddesses, carrying cornucopiae and offering bowls of fruit and grain to animals. The sovereign Cernunnos signifies generosity and magnanimity toward those he protects.

As early as the fourth century B.C., Cernunnos appears in rock drawings from the Camonica Valley of northern Italy. Cernunnos's authority is heralded by his great antlers, signifying his lordship among the animals of the forest of Europe. Through the centuries, his symbols—antlers of a great stag, Celtic jewelry called torcs, and the ram-horned snake—remained remarkably consistent.[56] Drawn on cave walls by Iron Age Celts, he appears robed and standing, and arrayed with great antlers, torcs on both arms, and a ram-horned snake at his side. On the Gundestrup Cauldron, Cernunnos's portrayal is regal: he sits cross-legged on the ground like a hunter, grasping a torc in one hand and a ram-horned snake against his face in the other. He is surrounded by a bull, hound, boar, and otherworldly animals. A stag (as in Oracle 22) with identical antlers stands beside him, as though mirroring his image as an animal.

Extending his sovereignty to include imagery usually associated with the mother goddesses, Roman-Celtic statues of Cernunnos show him carrying abundant cornucopiae, feeding animals, and offering grain or coins from a bag.[57] Like the mother goddess, also common at this time, Cernunnos extends his protection to include the growth of crops and the health and well-being of animals and humans alike.

His best-known image comes from Lady Charlotte Guest's rendering of "The Lady of the Fountain," included in her translation of the *Mabinogion*. Cernunnos appears as the potent Lord of the Animals:

> *Sleep here tonight, and in the morning arise early, and take the road upwards through the valley until thou . . . comest to a large sheltered glade with a mound in the centre. And thou wilt see a black man of great stature on the top of the mound. He is not smaller than two men of this world. He has but one foot, and one eye in the middle of his forehead. And he has a club of iron. . . . And he is not a comely man, but on the contrary he is exceedingly ill favoured; and he is the woodward of that wood.*

And thou wilt see a thousand wild animals grazing all around him. . . .

And the next morning I arose . . . and proceeded straight through the valley to that wood. . . . And there was I three times more astonished at the number of wild animals. . . . And the black man was there, sitting upon the top of the mound. Huge of stature as the man had told me. . . .

Then I asked him what power he had over the animals. . . . And he took his club in his hand, and with it he struck a stag so great a blow that it brayed vehemently, and at his braying the animals came together, as numerous as the stars in the sky, so that it was difficult for me to find room in the glade to stand among them. There were serpents, and dragons and divers sorts of animals. And [the black man] looked at them, and bade them go and feed; and they bowed their heads, and did him homage as vassals to their lord.[58]

IF YOU ARE DRAWN TO THIS ORACLE, you may not think of yourself as regal, as having a noble character; yet this capacity is developing within you. Others are already looking to you for strength, support, and guidance, even if you are not aware of your influence on them and your importance in their eyes. The "others" may be your children, employees, friends, partners, family, or neighbors. If you are not in a position of great external authority, your character is nonetheless leaving a strong impression on those around you. If your meditation has been strong, your spiritual maturity may be garnering such strength that it is beginning to show in your actions and presence.

Generosity comes from confidence and magnanimity from strength, an inner knowledge that life will always be filled up and replenished anew. More and more, your actions are spontaneous and unaffected. By responding to the needs of others unselfconsciously, you are participating in the natural urge of creation to increase in generosity and love.

~ 22 ~

Utterly Stag

WILD NATURE

Invoking the Union of Focus and Passion

The stag represents the wildness of nature. Associated with Cernunnos, the Lord of the Animals, and the goddesses of the sacred hunt, the stag acquired divine status among the Iron Age Celts. The stag's noble presence among the animals, its branching antlers resembling mature trees, and potency and aggression during the rutting season, epitomize the great forests of old Europe over which the stag presided as King of the Forest. The stag represents the noble and wild passions within all of nature.

In the Camonica Valley of northern Italy, cave walls contain rock drawings dating from the late Neolithic people through the Bronze and Iron Age Celts. The Celts were renowned hunters and their numerous stag images on cave walls indicate a reverence for the stag and an eagerness for the sacred hunt. Images from the fourth and seventh centuries portray staglike or antlered hunters, suggesting shape-shifting or, at least, an intimate correspondence with the quarry. Dominating over three-quarters of the religious imagery, drawings of the stag are often blended with another powerful Celtic image, the sun. At times, the rays of the sun appear as antlers, signifying a common sovereignty. Attesting to the stag's noble, if not divine, status, one rock drawing shows a circle of figures dancing or praying around a stag with tremendous antlers.[59]

A synthesis of archaeological and mythological evidence points to the stag as symbolizing wild nature, the King of the Forest. Ancient Gaul was heavily forested, as was England and Ireland. The stag's antlers branching like a tree into the sky, together with its speed, dignity, and carriage, imply a noble signature among the forest animals.[60]

Typically, the stag is associated in Celtic mythology with Cernunnos, the Lord of the Animals (Oracle 21). The Gundestrup Cauldron depicts an antlered Cernunnos with his familiar companion, the true stag.[61] Perhaps resplendent of an older tradition, goddesses are closely linked with the stag, especially when power and fertility are invoked. The Irish goddess Flidhais, who kept herds of deer as though they were cattle, seems to personify the wild and fertile nature of the surrounding forest. A goddess presiding over the sacred hunt of the stag was found buried with a Celtic warrior in an Iron Age site at Strettweg in Austria.[62]

Lastly, in the Christian era, the deer is associated with St. Patrick in Ireland: The king has sent men to ambush Patrick on every road leading to his court at Tara. Patrick passes the soldiers with his company of eight young clerics, followed by Benen carrying Patrick's writing tablets on his back. The men pass unnoticed, appearing as deer followed by a fawn with a white bird perched on its shoulder.[63]

IF YOU ARE DRAWN TO THIS ORACLE, you want to act from the passionate and spontaneous side of your nature. Yet your passions are still unruly, creating disorder within and around you. By bringing focus to your passions, you can harness the passionate and sometimes unruly forces within your own nature. Without this inner focus, even creative passions can generate tension and conflict. In emulating the quiet dignity and watchfulness of the stag, you can skillfully command your passions and create harmony in your life affairs.

The stag's sovereignty amid the wildness of nature is quiet, alert, and reserved—ample balance for the virility and power within. In walking quietly and attentively in danger, remaining calm and alert under stress, and meeting each situation with the right balance of speed and strength, the stag models inner and outer poise and self-control. A calm and steady focus will allow you to remain calm in any situation, as though you were walking serenely in a forest. However unruly your nature or the situation, a one-pointed focus will bring power and strength to your actions.

~ 23 ~

Ram-horned Snake

SHAPE-SHIFTING

Invoking the Quality of Shape-Shifting

The ram-horned snake is the Celts' most vigorous image of shape changing. The snake's form, consciousness, and action shift easily and spontaneously. Adorned with the powerful curling horns of the ram, the ram-horned snake brings together the regenerative and healing powers of the snake with the vigor, strength, and fertility of the ram. The ram-horned snake is particularly adept at responding swiftly to changing circumstances.

Shape-shifting, or shape changing, is remarkably common in the Celtic world. From archaeological finds of bas-reliefs depicting the ram-horned serpent of the Iron Age Celts to Irish and Welsh tales and legends of the great oral tradition, shape-shifting occurs frequently. Otherworldly beings, humans, and animals willfully change form when pursued and in danger, or seamlessly change from one form to another as acts of creation. Shape-shifting is the natural inheritance of otherworldly beings. The Welsh bard Taliesin tells of his multidimensional origins:

I have been in many shapes before I assumed a constant form:
I have been a narrow sword, a drop in the air; a shining bright star; a letter among words in the book of origins.
I have been lanternlight for a year and a day,
I have been a bridge spanning three score rivers.
I have flown as an eagle, been a coracle on the sea,
I have been a drop in a shower, a sword in battle, a string in a harp.
Nine years in enchantment, on water, in foam,
I have absorbed fire, I have been a tree in a covert,
There is nothing of which I have not been part.[64]

In domestic shrines of the earliest Celts to the medieval tales of wonder and adventure, a swift change in shape, consciousness, or action gives zest and adventure to the Celtic legends and way of life.

The ram-horned snake vividly portrays the prevalent capacity of beings in the Celtic world to shape-shift quickly and spontaneously. The natural capacity of the snake to renew life and the capacity of the ram to act with strength and authority are brought together in this uncanny and vibrant image of a snake adorned with the curling horns of a ram. In a striking portrayal in stone relief at Cirencester in Gloucestershire, England, the ram-horned snake is physically blended with an image of Cernunnos, the antlered Lord of the Animals (see Oracle 21):

"Cernunnos's body is merged with those of the two ram-horned snakes which replace his own legs and rear up on each side of his head to eat the fruit or grains clustered by his ears."[65]

If you are drawn to this oracle, you are urged to bring shape-shifting to some aspect of your life. A present situation may invite a change in attitude, action, or rearrangement of relationships, plans, logistics, or details. Depending on the situation, the changes may be crucial to many people or subtle, perceivable only to you. By sensing the opportune moment, spontaneous shifts in action, consciousness, and outward appearance may occur quickly and effortlessly. Making the same change later may require more time and effort. By shape-shifting now, you will begin to strengthen your capacity to shape-shift when the right circumstances occur in the future.

With practice and increased sensitivity, you can develop the skill of shape-shifting. From a spiritual perspective, as the boundaries between the realms of this middle world and the spirit world grow thinner, the extraordinary qualities of the animals and plants around you may become your expert teachers.

~ 24 ~

Banishing of Snakes

LOSS OF HOPE AND REGENERATIVE POWER

Invoking Breakthrough and Reconnection with the Natural World

The break in the connection with the powers of the Otherworld is symbolized in the banishing of the snakes, attributed to St. Patrick in Ireland. As snakes are a well-known symbol of the goddesses, especially mother goddesses such as Brigit, the popular belief in their banishment represents a break with the primal and regenerative authority of the earth and the Otherworld. The banishing of snakes signifies the loss of hope and regenerative power and invites reconnection.

Croagh Patrick in County Mayo is the traditional site associated with St. Patrick's banishing of the snakes from Ireland. The conical mountain, tipped with white quartz, stands majestically overlooking the Atlantic Ocean at Clew Bay. Also known as the Reek, the mountain commands attention and has been a site of religious activities since ancient times.

In a delightfully Irish manner, ancient and Christian traditions intertwine at Croagh Patrick. Some thirty thousand pilgrims still come annually to ascend the mountain, circuit the stations for prayer, or join the festivities on the first Sunday in August (or the last Sunday in July), the day traditionally associated with Lughnasa, the harvest festival in honor of the warrior god Lugh. By some reports, since the mountain is associated with fertility, even into the mid-nineteenth century only women were allowed to ascend the steep slope to the summit. There the women, and especially those who were childless, slept in the "bed" of the goddess in hope of obtaining fertility.[66]

Many legends associated with St. Patrick depict his struggle with a snake goddess, symbolizing Brigit (Oracle 7), and commonly known as the devil's mother, the Caora or the Caorthanach.[67] By tradition, the mountain goddess attacks Patrick as a great bird and later as a monstrous snake. He banishes her from the mountain, but she escapes to a lake at the side of the mountain, reappearing at Lough Derg, County Donegal, to attack Patrick once again.

If you are drawn to this oracle, you are probably experiencing a loss of energy, vitality, and generativity in the world. The Banishing of Snakes signifies a disconnection with the primal elements of the earth responsible for physical, emotional, and spiritual well-being. Disconnected in this way, your body tends to feel limp and lethargic, and your emotions are likely to be depressive.

Reestablishing a stable connection with the transformative powers of the Otherworld typically involves a lengthy and steady process of recovery. If severely depleted, your physical body and even your emotions may require a slow rhythm to heal and revitalize. You may also have to break strong personal habits that deplete your energy and health. Many factors are involved in this process, including attention to proper diet and exercise, adequate sleep and rest, time spent outdoors, and sustaining a nurturing social and emotional life. If you have a positive and appreciative attitude toward your natural environment, your recovery will be quicker and stronger. It may also be necessary to look at ways in which you may be dismissing your own physical and sexual needs or participating in addictive habits that undermine your physical and emotional vitality.

~ 25 ~

Oak

THE ANCIENT WOOD

Invoking the Qualities of Respect and Timelessness

Oaks are among the long-lived trees, signifying the presence of the ages and the long memory of trees. Elder oaks are revered as ancient goddesses residing upon the earth. In touching the sky with its branches and the Otherworld with its roots, oaks bring the forces of life and death together. Dead in winter and alive again in spring, oaks portray the steady passage of life. Symbolizing the connection of the Middle World with the forces of subterranean earth and sky, groves of aged oaks inspire celebration of the seamless continuity of life.

Like most other trees, the oaks are strongly associated with the goddesses. They symbolize the ceaseless passage of life from birth to death to life anew. Like the goddesses, they are connected through their roots to the Otherworld beneath the ground, where otherworldly spirits dwell. Stretching their branches into the sky, they are connected with the spirits of the Sky World, particularly Taranis (Oracle 58), the god of lightning and thunder. The older the oak, the more enchanted, numinous, and sacred it is.

Oaks were especially sacred to the druids. A natural grove of aged oaks draws the spirits of the Sky World and the Otherworld to the Middle World, the human and animal world residing on the ground. In ancient times, Celts worshiped in open-air groves throughout Europe and Asia Minor. Even the Romans were wary of them, fearing that oak groves were mysterious and dark.[68] Still dwelling among us in the Middle World, the aged oaks of our time invite us to their sacred grounds to connect with the spirits of both worlds and to celebrate the continuation of life throughout the ages.

The long life of oaks signifies the presence of the ages and the long memories of trees, spanning the ages. Oaks take us unto themselves as a precious creation, assuring us in their sway that life is knowledge enough. In a poem about a neighbor, a contemporary Irish poet, Cathal Ó Searcaigh, speaks to us of feeding "from the Tree of Knowledge":

She inclined to flesh but also to fun
And though she was fond of swearing and gap-toothed
She was never gruff or gloomy with us
When we visited her on Sundays
And she made us a drop of tea
While she hotly "dashed" this and "dratted" that. . . .

She kept herself there like a tree
growing and withering according to season
"It's not ageing I am, but ripening."

and her words fell like seeds into the
welcoming earth of my mind.
And when she'd wrap me in her limbs so tightly,
I felt the fat—the growth rings of her body.[69]

IF YOU ARE DRAWN TO THIS ORACLE, the venerable oaks inspire respect for their continuity of life within change and chaos. You are called to a deep remembering of who you are.

For the venerable oaks, time is holy, every moment. Every memory has its place. Celebration and ritual inspire vision and perspective. Wherever you live, being in nature, especially among aged trees, may be cause for remembering—not because memories are necessarily pleasurable, but because they are ripe for the harvest of discovery. Amid the vicissitudes and changes of life, all mystical paths invite deep remembering. In the long memory of trees, no memory, however distant, is ever lost. You and your life in its deepest reflections are memories held forever. Perhaps you have separated yourself from deep memories of who you are or from the life of your family or community, or separated yourself from particular memories. Still, the aged oaks cradle them as though they are treasures for unpacking.

Deep remembering ultimately leads to a sense of peace and continuity. From the context of continuity, present circumstances—the good and ill alike—appear like snapshots on a long and special journey.

~ 26 ~

Rowan, Mountain Ash

THE ALCHEMICAL WAND

Invoking the Qualities of Otherworldly Protection

The rowan tree and its winter clusters of red berries signify the protection of the Otherworld within the human middle world. A rowan branch above the door protects homes from unwanted intruders, especially mischievous spirits. A small rowan twig concealed underneath garments protects the wearer while traveling. Eating the red berries of an enchanted rowan brings wisdom. But beware, a fire of rowan wood may entreat the presence of otherworldly spirits, both gentle and malevolent.

The rowan tree or mountain ash is honored throughout the Celtic world for its role in the magic and enchantments emanating from the Otherworld. Its aspect can be potent and fierce. In the mythological cycle of Irish tales, Etáin is struck with a "wand of scarlet rowan berries" and instantly disappears into a pool of water.[70] In the Fionn Cycle of Irish tales, the hero Finn acquires understanding of all things by eating a red-speckled salmon that fed on the berries of the enchanted rowan tree overhanging the pool (see Oracle 20).

Rowan trees are favored because they provide chthonic or otherworldly protection and good luck. People like to have one neighboring the house and holy places or to secretly fasten small twigs to their clothes to bring good luck. A rowan branch above the door protects the home from fire and unkindly intruders and spirits. In a story collected in the last century in the lowlands of Scotland, the rowan protects the peasantry while watching the procession of faeries, which takes place at the coming of summer. From beneath a door arrayed with rowan branches, they can safely "gaze on the cavalcade, as with music sounding, bridles ringing, and voices mingling, [as] it pursued its way from place to place."[71]

Rowan berries and rowan branches are the certain protectors of cows, sacred to the goddesses of the underworld. Rowan are kept in the barn "to safeguard the cows; put in the pail and around the churn to ensure that the profit of the milk [is] not stolen."[72] In a story told in County Cavan in the 1940s, Charles King relays that the "old people would tie roundberry [rowanberry] to the cows' tails. They would make a small ring of the roundberry and tie it with a red rag, and slip it in as far as they could on the cow's tail. . . . That was done as a 'protection' against the butter being taken from the milk during the year."[73]

Rowan wood also serves in divination. It is likely that the Norse carved runes from rowan wood. A rowan wand is used in divining the future. A fire of rowan wood casts spells and anticipates danger by summoning underworldly spirits, not all of them benevolent.

IF YOU ARE DRAWN TO THIS ORACLE, the protection and good luck of the rowan are being offered to you. Are you presently engaged in challenging or risky situations that beg extra protection and comfort? Do circumstances or the time of year invite circumspection and care? Do you feel any need to shield yourself from the unkindness of others or from spirits in the psychic realm? The presence of the rowan suggests both caution in worldly affairs and the protection of unseen forces. Its otherworldly authority dispels fear and anxiety, enabling life to proceed beneficially.

It may be an auspicious time to consider and appreciate the chthonic forces at hand in your life. Such forces stir within the human realm, bringing vitality and even healing and guidance. In the slow, steady pace of the underworld, you may be dreaming or "seeing" in new ways, prompted by otherworldly forces stirring within your unconscious mind. In this way, the presence of the rowan is a means of divining your next step, goal, relationship, or endeavor. Usually, there is no great drama or vision, just a gentle and pervasive shift in perspective and inclination. Like the rowan's red berries in winter, changes accord with the rhythms of nature.

~ 27 ~

Hazel

THE DIVINING ROD

Invoking Concentration and Reflection

The hazel tree symbolizes purity and virtue, and by inference guidance. The green and edible hazelnut yields a milky substance signifying an ancient association with the mother goddesses of fertility, healing, and sources of knowledge. Its gentle branches and foliage lend an aspect of ease and tranquillity. The hazel's naturally forking branches are especially favored in divining underground sources of water. Practical in nature, the hazel provides guidance and direction in the practical concerns of everyday life.

The hazel tree is comforting and soothing by nature. Its gentle canopy lends an aspect of ease and tranquillity. While the otherworldly aspects of the rowan tree are associated with fierce chthonic goddesses, the hazel is associated with the gentler and nourishing aspects of the mother goddesses. Its presence brings a sense of security and ease, like a healing ointment stroked on dry and thirsty skin. The hazel signals attentiveness to the practical and domestic concerns of life, including our health, well-being, sustenance, and relations with family and friends.

The motherly aspects of the hazel are enhanced by the milk found in the green nut of the hazel. The hazelnut, therefore, signifies purity, and through its virtue, the giving of guidance to others.

Among the Fianna of Ireland in the Finn Cycle, only the noblest, swiftest, and most honorable men were chosen as comrades-in-arms. Tested first for honor and for proficiency in poetry, the warriors were finally tested for their strength in the fury of battle. While carrying only a shield and hazel branch and standing in a meadow, the warrior faces a hail of spears thrown by nine comrades. It is a ludicrously unfair assault if the warrior doesn't trust in himself and the virtue of the hazel.[74]

The use of hazel branches by water diviners is the hazel's best-known quality. For centuries, the naturally forking branches of the hazel tree have been used by diviners to search for underground sources of water (and some say for ley lines as well). By gently holding the two ends of a forked hazel branch at arm's length and scanning the ground with it, the pointing rod drops suddenly toward the ground, thus marking the source of underground water. Its signal is clear and directed. The stronger the pull, the closer the water is to the surface. Through the ages, the hazel's divining properties have been connected to divination and guidance.

The hazel may also have been used in rites of divination by employing a cracked nut as an oracle. While the sources of this ritual are scarce and uncertain, nonetheless the hazel is favored as a source of knowledge and guidance in the common and pragmatic aspects of living.

IF YOU ARE DRAWN TO THIS ORACLE, the presence of the hazel tree directs you to the natural world for instruction. The hazel usually brings clarity by encouraging you to seek the inner meaning of events, relations, and situations. Looking at the surface of events will not help. However, calm reflection may reveal an inner meaning, significance, pattern, or growth that is not apparent on the surface of things. You may find yourself drawn into a period of quiet reflection, rather than activity and strategizing. The hazel will gently support your reflection, meditation, concentration, or prayer. Since the hazel tree encourages deep serenity and quietude, it may be an especially auspicious time for taking a vacation alone or going on retreat.

A hazel tree, and especially the hazelnut, signify the search of the inner world for guidance concerning your everyday affairs. Its signals are often found in nature. Like a Celtic hermit, you might look for guidance from the actions of the birds and creatures around you. The sudden appearance of certain animals and their habits and qualities, for example, may direct you to aspects of your own nature important to your personal development. Seek quietude, then wait and watch.

~ 28 ~

Thorn Tree

THE SACRED SIGN

Invoking Purity of Intentions and Actions

A faery thorn is sacred and inviolable, as it marks the habitats of faeries, especially a solitary bush growing by itself in an open field. Cutting down a faery thorn brings calamity and misfortune for dishonoring the habitats of the neighboring faeries. By honoring the sacred thorn, the people of the Middle World acquire the skills for attending and protecting the sanctity of all aspects of life, and they grow in wisdom.

The faery thorn tree or bush reminds us of the presence of the faeries living nearby. The thorn tree marks the habitats of the faeries, and the surrounding ground is hallowed by the thorn. The proverbial wisdom tells us that it is plain foolishness to cut or damage a thorn tree, especially a solitary thorn growing alone in an open space, marking the boundary between neighbors, near a sacred well, faery rath (fort), or home. Even "city people" provide little courtyards amid urban complexes for lonely thorns, fearing to incur the wrath of the faeries. No small wonder, as tradition has it, that cutting a thorn tree is met with disaster, and even death. Nearly everywhere in rural Ireland, the story is told of a local man who ignored the advice of his neighbors, cut down a thorn tree, and died shortly thereafter.[75]

A recent and well-known incident occurred in County Antrim, as told by Jim Grant of Belfast. Some years ago, during the construction of an immense factory, a thorn tree remained untouched by the workers. The local "boys" cleared everything else, but they would not

> *chop it down or interfere with it in any way. The company finally got an Englishman to remove it. He chopped the tree down and bulldozed the roots. The next stage was putting in the piles, concrete pilings which were approximately 12 inches in diameter and 10 feet long—to give foundation. They laid the first of the foundation with a pile driver, but when they returned the next morning, the pilings were three feet from where they should have been! . . . So, they got a new length of piles and again placed them in the ground. The next morning, the pilings were three feet from their original locations, but in the opposite direction of the first move! So they called a conference to see who was guilty. . . . The smallest man in the meeting, he stood up and said, "The only way you are going to build your factory here is to replace our tree where it was." So they*

> *said to him, "How can we, if it has been cut?" He said, "Get it grafted." Nobody believed him initially, of course. . . . So, they brought a tree specialist from Holland in. He replanted the roots on the tree and grafted it. There is now a wee courtyard in the middle of the factory, with a thorn tree growing. The faery man was never seen again, but the thorn tree thrives.*[76]

By tradition, the thorn tree blooms on the first day of May, signaling the coming of summer. Always liking a good party, the faeries may favor the thorn, not only for its fierce, protecting thorns, but for the merry-making that comes with summer.

IF YOU ARE DRAWN TO THIS ORACLE, the thorn tree asks you to purify actions and intentions, including purifying those of the past. The thorn tree is sacred and inviolate. It sets a very high standard and should never be disturbed in any way. Impure actions and ill intentions, however minor, harm other forms of life as well as yourself, both outwardly and inwardly. Living in accord with the actions of nature, which sustains all life impartially, is to live humbly and richly, gently and courageously, in the giving and receiving of life. The purity of your actions and intentions, rather than how others think or feel about you, sets your course toward well-being and the acquiring of wisdom.

The presence of the thorn tree reminds you that all aspects of your life are sacred. Take time to reflect on what you may be overlooking or ignoring in your life. When you identify it, pay attention and protect it. Remember that the thorn tree is among the humblest-looking of trees and that some of the most precious aspects of your life may not be immediately apparent.

~ 29 ~

Leprechauns

EARTH

Invoking the Qualities of Playfulness and Mirth

The leprechaun is a small, mischievous, and wizened man who often appears dressed in fanciful clothes such as a red vest, green trousers, and a conical hat. Aligned with the otherworldly powers of the subterranean earth, he knows its hidden treasures and is therefore very rich. When encountered cobbling in a lonely place, humans torment him to relinquish his golden guinea purse or lead them to a crock of gold. Through cleverness and trickery, he typically outwits his captors and escapes.

The leprechaun is known by many local names throughout Ireland. All manner of similar dwarves and gnomes inhabit the stories of western Europe, especially Germany and France, particularly Celtic Brittany in France. The leprechaun often lives in the ground or in rock caverns and caves. Though commonly connected with the faeries or known as the cobbler to the faeries, the leprechaun is a singular otherworldly being associated with the underground and its riches, especially gold and hidden treasure.

Most commonly, a leprechaun appears as a small and mischievous man, a wee cobbler, who possesses an inexhaustible purse of golden coins or hidden treasure. Typically encountered at the thresholds of time, just before dawn or after night has fallen, a leprechaun will often be dressed like a country gentleman of the last century, wearing a fanciful red vest with gold buttons or a gentleman's dress coat with large buttons, tight-fitting trousers or knee-breeches, and curious shoes with large metal buckles or boots with curled-up and pointed toes. Occasionally, a leprechaun will befriend a poor farmer or a child by leading them to hidden treasure or leaving a guinea in an old chest each night. Some leprechauns live merrily in the wine cellars of old and noble families—as long as good wine is kept in the cellar. Nonetheless, most leprechauns are seen cobbling a single shoe in a hedgerow or out in the bog.[77] When chased, he may disappear as though swallowed by the ground.

A common leprechaun story tells of a man, or occasionally a woman, who catches a leprechaun cobbling on a single shoe and makes a "close prisoner" of him. Until he tells where the gold is, the leprechaun has no chance of getting away. Taking the man out to an old ring fort where the faeries live, the leprechaun shows him a big ragwort, and says, "Dig under this weed tomorrow morning and you'll get a crock of gold." "Wait," he says, "and we'll mark it. Take off my red garter and tie it around the [ragwort], and you'll know where to dig in the morning." The man does exactly that and lets the wee man go. When he comes out in the morning, there is a red garter on every ragwort in the field, thousands of them, exactly the same size and pattern.[78]

Even with a tight grasp about a leprechaun, the wee man can only be trapped by an unbroken stare. Many stories of leprechauns tell of his imitating a lover's voice from behind, alerting the captor to some alleged danger, creating a ruckus, and the like. A likely story from Ireland goes like this:

> *The* clocharachán *[a local name for a leprechaun] makes shoes inside a little rock cavern and he has* sparán na scillinge: *every time you'd look in the purse there would be a shilling there. You'd seldom see the* clocharachán *and it is very difficult to catch him. A man heard that he was in some rock cavern or other. He came upon him one evening and gripped him firmly.*
>
> *"Give me your purse!" said the man.*
>
> *"Let me go," said the* clocharachán, *"and I'll give you the purse."*
>
> *If you took your eye off him he'd get away from you.*
>
> *"Get a red-hot spit," said the* clocharachán, *"and stick it in his backside!"*
>
> *The man looked all around him and the* clocharachán *departed and took his purse away with him!*[79]

IF YOU ARE DRAWN TO THIS ORACLE, you are attracting the playful and resourceful qualities of the earth. The leprechaun is boundlessly rich. Each time he opens his silken purse, he finds another golden guinea. Yet his presence often has a double meaning. On the one hand, he beckons the rich resources of the earth toward you, tempts you, and may bountifully reward you. On the other hand, he often turns your attachment toward wealth into a standing joke in which you are the principal player.

The presence of this oracle suggests that you are being tempted by material resources in the form of money, great opportunities, or a "deal." These material resources may come, but more likely, they are ephemeral. Being a natural trickster and mischief-maker, there is no telling what the leprechaun's influence will be. There is no human logic predicting his rare gifts of hidden treasure. There is only a slim hope that your present circumstances will result in making you rich or famous.

Spiritually, the tempting yet ephemeral riches of the leprechaun invite you to cultivate detachment and equanimity with regard to material treasure.

~ 30 ~

Faery Wind

AIR

Invoking Exchange with the Spirit World

The whirlwinds of late summer are the faery hosts out making their rounds. The whirlwinds come on the loveliest days of late summer at harvest time. Sweeping everything into their path, they pass over the countryside as if searching for hay, corn, or even animals. Haystacks are hit and lifted into the skies. Heaps of corn disappear into the faery winds. Sometimes men and women out harvesting blow away, too. The faery hosts raise the high winds to take what they need.

In Ireland, the old people say that it is the faery hosts who raise the high winds. Nodding their heads or tipping their caps at the wind as if greeting a lady, a small whirlwind is thought to be "the gentry," the faeries making their customary rounds about the countryside. A high wind, though, is fearsome and unlucky. Even if you are not blown away, it is unlucky to get a "blast." Grazing horses are known to snort to blow the "good people" out of their way. A characteristic story comes from County Donegal:

> *I myself have seen a faery whirlwind on a summer day take all the hay of a holding into the firmament. They often raised high winds in harvest-time to get the corn they wanted. One year long ago a man named Paddy Bhride living east of here at Fál Garbh had the devil's own lot of corn sown—as much as the rest of the townland all together. When he had all his corn reaped and stooked there came a nigh of high wind and Paddy went out [and] there was not as much left as would sprinkle Holy Water on a corpse.*[80]

The faery hosts raise the high winds to take what they need of the harvest. As the winds sweep across the winnowed fields, they suddenly can pull a haystack into the sky. A man or woman, horses, and cows can be swept away, too. Sometimes the faeries speak or laugh as they pass across the fields, departing with an acerbic bit of faery whimsy:

> *One fine autumn day long ago, a gang of men were reaping oats, and three women were binding the oats after them. They heard a whirlwind coming into the field with force. The women stood looking at the whirlwind. It was lifting the oats, taking it up into the sky, and whirling and whirling all the time. One of the women stooped, and pulled a wisp of grass from the side of the ridge, and when the whirlwind was making for them: "Here," she said, on purpose, "take that instead of me!" throw-*

ing the wisp at it. "Aw," said the whirlwind, "you grey goose's shit, it wasn't you I was after!"[81]

IF YOU ARE DRAWN TO THIS ORACLE, your life will be enhanced by giving your money, resources, and time to worthy charitable and spiritual endeavors. Within the Christian tradition, tithing is a traditional—and often misunderstood—term for giving back to creation from the fruits of your labors. Numerous indigenous cultures have elaborate rituals for redistributing wealth. In many of the world's religious traditions, merit is acquired by honoring holy men and women with food and alms. In this oracle, the faery winds signify the otherworldly taking of a portion of the harvest to support the needs of the spirit world.

Because the spirit world constantly acts on your behalf, it is honorable to return a measure of your resources to it and to those who support prayerful and spiritual activities on your behalf. The faery winds urge us to avoid indulgence and to cultivate less attachment to material possessions. By consciously giving of your money and time, a natural sense of exchange and respect for the spirit world and all life will gradually extend to everything you do.

~ 31 ~

Willy the Wisp—Jack O' Lantern

FIRE

Invoking the Use of Creativity and Talent

Willy the Wisp was a poor and quick-witted man who ill used his talents taunting his neighbors, including the devil. Some say he was an awful man who always got the upper hand with his neighbors, and even with the devil. When Willy died, he was welcome neither in heaven nor hell. He still wanders about the Irish bogs at night with a lantern or his nose afire. His presence signifies the fires of creativity and talent and their right use in the world.

Mysterious lights are seen on the bogs in Ireland at night. Holding a wisp, a lantern, or with his own nose ablaze to illumine his way in the dark, poor Willy the Wisp (also known as Jack O' Lantern) forever wanders the countryside. "Willy the Wisp . . . refused admittance of heaven and hell, was given a wisp for light by the devil. And Willy goes about lonesome places from that day to this and the wisp with him."[82] Willy the Wisp was too bad for heaven and too clever for hell.

When alive, he had been a terrible bad man who played spiteful tricks on his neighbors. His wicked eye was said to have the power to turn a person into a goat.[83] Carried away with his own cleverness, though, he taunted the devil and

> *got the upper hand of Old Nick in every deal. At long last he died and was sent down to hell. When the devil saw him coming he ordered all the doors and windows to be securely locked and bolted. Poor Will walked up and down expecting to be let in at any moment. Losing patience at long last he went over and began peeping in through the bars. What do you say if his nose didn't catch fire! But [he had] no [chance] of getting in. The poor fellow had to come back to Ireland and he is wandering up and down the country ever since with the tip of his nose on fire. That's the light you see when he's crossing the bog. . . . The fire on the tip of his nose is so strong that all the water in the ocean wouldn't extinguish it. He'll be wandering about night after night till Doomsday and then if the devil doesn't let him in I don't know what will become of him.*[84]

Never follow Willy's meandering light in the bog. He will lead a man or woman astray!

IF YOU ARE DRAWN TO THIS ORACLE, your creativity and talent may be going astray. A wise person uses his or her creativity wisely and unselfishly. Are you undervaluing your talents and skills and therefore undermining your endeavors? Are you withholding your strengths?

hoarding them? trivializing them? neglecting them? overlooking their potential and not attending to their development? Are you supporting your talents through proper diet, exercise, and rest?

Unwise or selfish use of creativity and talents brings misfortune. Wise and generous use of talents brings peace of mind and contentment. Compassionate use of talents brings much joy to the heart. In seeking to develop your talents and how to use them it is wise to seek guidance from those who have manifested their own talents in creative and generous ways. Such guidance will be inspiring and sound, because it is based on having already wrestled with the tensions of ambition and impatience, success and failure, giving and receiving, and passion and resistance.

~ 32 ~

Mermaids and Selkies

WATER

Invoking the Qualities of Longing and Wonder

Oracles and tales of mermaids and selkies bring the qualities of the depths of the sea to the depths of the human spirit: they convey femininity, beauty, and wonder into everyday life. Arising from palaces beneath the sea and coming ashore into our earthly realms, mermaids and selkies represent the alluring, mysterious, and unknown qualities evoked by the sea. Mermaids and selkies especially represent the depths of human longing for fulfillment and wonder in our lives.

The selkie or sea woman of Celtic lore is beautiful, wistful, and enchanting. As she is combing her long, lustrous hair atop a rock on the rocky coasts of Ireland or Scotland, a lone fisherman encounters her and steals her magic cloak or cap. Unable to return to the sea without the cloak, she is stranded ashore and follows the man to his home. Though captured and melancholy for her palace and children beneath the sea, she often grows fond of the fisherman who found her ashore and provides for her. As man and woman, they live an enchanted life and bear human children who sometimes have exceptional qualities. The sea woman is supernatural and he is human; she is wild and he is tamed; she is unknown and he is familiar; she is a creature of the sea and he a denizen of the land. Eventually finding her cloak hidden in the roof thatching or hay rick and often aided by her children, she wordlessly hastens to the sea. Always returning to the sea, she occasionally returns to land to provide for her children—but only when the fisherman is out to sea. The enchantment gone and his life again tame and familiar, the man wistfully yearns for her to return to his household and bed.

Is it not hard for me to speak of love, an affliction from which
I cannot be relieved?
There's not one in the place who knew my situation but would
loudly lament for me;
It is hard for me to maintain my love for the maiden of the
treasures who was not of human descent,
And were you to raise your hand and save me from death I
would never take anyone but you.[85]

IF YOU ARE DRAWN TO THIS ORACLE, you are called to re-invoke or re-enchant some aspect of your life with longing and wonder. In some way you may be feeling bored, tamed, captured by circumstance, or disenchanted with some aspect of your life. You may be longing for the unfamiliar, the enigmatic, the mysterious, and the yet-to-be-discovered aspects of life. You might wish to seek inspiration from the unknown and unexplored aspects of your life. Male or female, the depths of your femininity, especially its more exotic qualities, may be longing for attention and exploration. You may be unusually attracted to beauty. You are encouraged to explore the mysterious aspects of your life, to puzzle over unknowns without trying to analyze them, and to allow bewilderment and wonder to be your guides. The mermaid's allure is her mystery from the depths of the sea.

Part Three

Oracles from the Otherworld

Those oracles relating to:

The Earth and the Fiery Otherworld

Gateways to the Otherworld

Beings Between the Worlds

The Faery World

~ 33 ~

Sovereignty

VOLUPTUOUS AUTHORITY

Invoking the Vitality of the Natural World

The sovereignty of the earth is personified by the mother goddesses who pass sovereignty to rightful kings. The earth's power originates in her mysterious and fiery interior, giving the earth's surface its lively, sensuous, and voluptuous qualities. The earth's hot interior rises to caress the earth's surface through wells and thermal springs, seas and lakes, certain mountains and hills, and in the essence or power of place. Sovereignty signifies the fresh vitality of the natural world.

The sovereignty of the earth expresses herself in the wonders of the natural world, its beauty, intricacies, and marvels stroking the senses and calling us homeward to the present moment in time. Celtic sovereignty is scarcely a transcendent deity, but queenly and earthy, naming us kin and returning us to the soil that bore us into flesh. The earth herself pulses with the power of creation. Thermal waters rush to her surface, her sacred cauldrons boiling within.

As in most cultures with an ancient lineage, the Celts revere the earth and personify her as mother, the source of life. The goddess Brigit of Oracle 7 carries the clearest attributes of sovereignty in several Celtic countries. Sovereignty is passed, albeit temporarily, to the rightful king or chief of Oracle 14. In Britain, she is worshiped as Brigantia, a territorial goddess and namesake of a Celtic tribe once living in the Midlands. In the preparations for celebrating the Feast of the Bride on February 1, a home-crafted symbol of sovereignty, a "small straight white wand (the bark being peeled off), [is placed] beside the figure [of Brigit]. The wand is generally of birch, broom, bramble, white willow, or other sacred wood. . . . A similar rod was given to the kings of Ireland at their coronation, and to the Lords of the Isles [of Scotland] at their instatement."[86] Similarly, Brigit is linked with the source of life and the seasons. According to Celtic lore, the serpent of the Otherworld resides within the earth, appearing on the Feast of the Bride after the harshness of winter is spent and the greening of spring begins.[87] Heavy with sleep in winter and restive and awake in spring, Brigit rules the seasons with her activities. She is sovereign.

If you are drawn to this oracle, you not only want to be out-of-doors but want the freshness and spontaneity of nature as a core dynamic in your everyday life. The raw and voluptuous quality of nature seems like fire to your physical well-being. Activities such as sitting in the sunshine, feeling the wind against your face, listening to the call of birds and the sounds of animals, crackling autumn leaves under your feet, or swimming with the current of a river are needs that seem to course like a stream through your muscles and nerves. It is not just the vigor of nature that attracts you, but the fresh and startling impetus in the acts of nature that spark your drive, health, and vitality.

It is best to catch the wind of this fiery energy while you can. Like weather and seasons, it changes. Now is an excellent time to play, to be spontaneous, and to allow your enthusiasm to guide you. Put your productivity agenda aside. Later, in a slower time, you can reflect and integrate.

~ 34 ~

Power of Place

CALLING IN THE SPIRIT OF PLACE

Invoking the Qualities of Familiarity, Remembrance, and Continuity

The Celts often name a place for its qualities and lore—a dell for providing shelter, a marshy corner for its soft and rushy bottom, a ring fort to signal an otherworldly ambiance, a meadow to mark the battles fought, or a holy well for its protectress. Affecting recollection, familiar places help us to situate ourselves in the passage of time and locale. Recalling such a place, Irish poet Cathal Ó Searcaigh concludes: "Contradictions are cancelled on the spot."[88]

The landscape—its rocky slopes, the forks of a river, an elder tree, a spring at its source, a widening plain, or undulating hills—reveals the features of the body of the mother earth, the goddess herself. Her countenance is found in the physical appearance of each place. The power of each place is utterly unique, so that its physiognomy and stories, so familiar, are wedded to the memory of the men and women living there. In Ireland and other Celtic lands, power implicit in the stones and earth of a place is frequently distilled in place names, recollecting in a word or phrase the deeds and fortunes of memories past. Like tonic to the human spirit, the power of place—in all its nuances, the horrific and foreboding, the beautiful and innocent—links individuals and community to lore and locale.

In discussing a genre of Irish literature known as *dindseanchas*, the poet Seamus Heaney writes that its poems and tales "relate the meanings of place names and constitute a form of mythological etymology . . . marr[ying] the geographical country with the country of the mind."[89] Heaney continues:

> *The landscape was sacramental, instinct with signs, implying a system of reality beyond the visible realities. Only thirty years ago, and thirty miles from Belfast, I experienced this kind of world vestigially and as a result may have retained some vestigial sense of place as it was experienced in the older dispensation. As I walked to school, I saw Lough Beg from Mulholland's Brae, and the spire of Church Island rose out of the trees. On Church Island Sunday in September, there was a pilgrimage out to the island, because St. Patrick was supposed to have prayed there, and prayed with such intensity that he branded the shape of his knee into a stone in the old churchyard. The rainwater that collected in that stone, of course, had healing powers, and the thorn bush beside it was pennanted with the rags used by those who rubbed their warts and sores in that*

water. . . . That legend, and the ringing ascetic triumph of rising in the frosts of winter to pray . . . all combined to give Slemish a nimbus of its own.[90]

The power of place is so intimate and "self-contained" that it is virtually hidden from those who inhabit the home, the locale, the village, or the city. Entering the place, the stranger "is immediately aware of the otherness and the intimate nature of the 'place.' One senses the odors unique to the place—its sounds and artifacts. . . . It is this quality of intimacy, based on uniqueness, that provides the possibility for placehood."[91] By intertwining landscape and lore, the power of place connects the human psyche within the nexus of time and space.

IF YOU ARE DRAWN TO THIS ORACLE, you are yearning for a place you can call your own, perhaps a home, a village, a region or country, or a community. You seem to want somewhere to root, to settle, and invest yourself fully. Not anywhere will do. The place must be uniquely right for you. The power of the place compels you. Its atmosphere, physical features, people, vegetation, smells, and wildlife attract you. It may be where you are but your psyche has not yet fully engaged it. It may be a place deeply familiar and redolent of personal memories. Wherever this place is, you are more fully alive there, as though the outer landscape mirrors the inner landscape of who you are and who you are becoming. This remarkable correspondence brings vitality and a sense of contentment and well-being.

Over the course of life, there are times to take pilgrimages to distant places and to garner their qualities to yourself. At other times, such as now, you are invited to situate your life in a particular place, to settle in and to mature amid the familiarity and memories built up over time. Surrounded by these intimacies as though encircled by the lacework of your life, your inner life and external surroundings blend together in support of each other.

~ 35 ~

Spirit of Mountains

BREASTS OF THE GODDESS

Invoking the Qualities of Impartiality and Forgiveness

Known as the Paps of Anu, two symmetrical, rounded mountains lie close together on the plains near Killarney in the Province of Munster in Ireland. Suggesting an ageless ritual, twentieth-century pilgrims carry stones from the bottom to the top of the mountains and then place the stones on the summits, forming unmistakable nipples on the breasts of the goddess. The strength of the goddess is her certain impartiality and forgiveness.

The Book of the Invasions, chronicling the successive invasions of Ireland, recounts stories of the Tuatha Dé Danann, the people of the goddess Anu, Áine, or Danu, who inhabited Ireland before the Celtic invasions from continental Europe. Initially from Galicia in northwestern Spain, the invading Celts compelled the Tuatha Dé to relinquish the Middle World and inhabit the Otherworld. Mythic history recounts the Tuatha Dé as a supernatural, godlike race having druids and poets of their own and hurling "a wind of wizards" against the Celts while still at sea.

> *The druids of [the Tuatha Dé Danann of] Ireland and the poets sang spells behind them, so that they were carried far from Ireland, and were in distress by reason of the sea. . . . And the wind rose against the ship wherein were Donn and Airech, two sons of Míl, and ship wherein were Bres, Búas, and Buaighne; so that they were drowned at the Sandhills at Tech Duinn.*[92]

The Tuatha Dé are identified with the goddess Anu, an ancestral mother goddess of Ireland. Anu was undoubtedly a fertility goddess associated with the land. Little else is known, though her Neolithic origins suggest solar attributes, linking the fecundity of the earth and the fertility of the sun.[93] One of her places of habitation, recorded in *The Book of the Invasions*, and an ancient center of ritual activity, is the Paps of Anu, a set of two breastlike mountains lying close together on gently rolling lowlands in County Kerry.[94] Modern-day pilgrims carry stones from the plains below to the very top of the mounds of stones left by pilgrims before them. Viewed even at a short distance, these mounds (probably ancient burial mounds) embellish the Paps of Anu with nipples (*paps* means breasts or teats). Below, near a natural spring and a starting point for ascending one of the paps, a shrine dedicated to the Virgin Mary beautifies a small clearing where the villagers still gather for occasional mass and festivals in midsummer.

IF YOU ARE DRAWN TO THIS ORACLE, you are invited to let go of judging yourself or others harshly. While corrective actions are essential in the course of human life, needlessly blaming yourself or others for past actions is neither practical nor life-sustaining. However awkward or painful, both seeking and extending forgiveness frees life to be lived more fully in the present.

The image of the breasts of the goddess signifies the nourishment of a mother's milk. The image overflows with the milk of blessing. Her capacity for bestowing mercy and forgiveness is boundless. As though untouched by human logic, she gives impartially to the just and unjust alike. You are encouraged to partake of her wisdom in some aspect of your life. Rather than judging or holding court on the actions of others (or of yourself), you may wish to reevaluate and amend those aspects of your life in which a gentler and more forgiving approach would be freeing and deeply gratifying in the long run.

~ 36 ~

Cauldron of the Otherworld

ALCHEMY

Invoking Healing and Replenishing the Spirit

The brewing cauldron resides in the Otherworld and appears on the earth to heal and give wisdom. In her semblance as a hag, the goddess tends the cauldron, adding elements of the earth and stars to preserve the ancient brew. Mythological warriors traveled to the Otherworld to seize the sacred chalice or cauldron to convey it to the Middle World. The Cauldron of the Otherworld symbolizes the goddess's powers of healing and replenishment to everyday life.

The cauldron conveys gifts from the Otherworld to restore health, replenish vitality, and grant wisdom and prophesy. It derives its supernatural power from the womb of the goddess, the inexhaustible cauldron of creation (Oracle 2). Through the art of alchemy and healing, the brewing cauldron of the Otherworld brings healing to creatures of the Middle World, or those dwelling on the earth.

Archaeological evidence and mythology portray cauldrons, pots, buckets, chalices, and vats as sacred symbols indicating replenishment, prosperity, and abundance. Precious objects including brooches, weapons, shields, and cauldrons—cast as offerings—have been found in lakes and at the source of springs. Domestic and temple statues found in Britain, France, and Germany frequently portray the Celtic goddesses Rosmerta and Nantosuelta, and occasionally their consorts Sucellus and Mercury, as holding or accompanied by various bowls, pots, and goblets. In the wine-producing regions along the Rhone and Rhine Rivers, the containers seem to hold wine, a supernatural elixir associated with the blood of birth and regeneration.[95] In Irish and Welsh myth and legend, cauldrons and chalices appear frequently as symbols of replenishment, rebirth, and inspiration. In the story of Taliesin's origins, as retold here by John Matthews, Ceridwen the Hag brews a supernatural potion for her son:

> *In the time of Arthur there lived in the region of Llyn Tegrid a nobleman named Tegid Foel [the Bald]. And he had a wife who was named Ceridwen, who was skilled in the magical arts. Tegrid and Ceridwen had two children: one who was so ugly that they called him Morfran [Great Crow]. . . . The other child was a daughter, whose name was Creirwy [Dear One], and she was as fair as Morfran was dark. Ceridwen thought that her son would never be accepted in the world because of his hideous looks . . . so she resolved to boil a Cauldron of Inspiration and Wisdom according to the Books of the Fíerllt, and the method of it was this: she must first gather certain*

herbs on certain days and hours, and put them in the Cauldron, which must then be kept boiling for a year and a day, until three drops of Inspiration were obtained.[96]

IF YOU ARE DRAWN TO THIS ORACLE, you are likely to attract the return of health, vitality, and optimism to your life. If you have been feeling weary, ill, or depressed, you are likely to feel more active, energetic, confident, and cheerful in the weeks ahead. The brewing cauldron signifies the potential to heal and replenish your emotional and spiritual well-being.

Spiritually, the presence of the brewing cauldron signals the return of elements of your essential nature that have been lost through harmful, neglectful, or wrong actions in the past. In the days and weeks ahead, you may recall personal qualities and hopes long abandoned. Some may have been cast off in childhood by trauma or disappointments. Others may have been left undeveloped, or discarded as impractical, ridiculous, frivolous, or childish. Still others may have been corrupted through lies and self-deceit. Having drawn this oracle, some of these qualities and hopes may now be returning to you.

~ 37 ~

Nymphs

HEALING

Invoking the Qualities of

Intimate and Loving Attention

Healing springs are associated with the healing properties of youthful goddesses, commonly personified as young, playful nymphs. Pilgrims gather around the bubbling waters, making prayers and offerings to a favored goddess. Children and adults bathe in the curative pools. Women sleep near pools thought to cure barrenness and convey fertility. The best-known nymph is Coventina, who signifies loving and healing attention to our physical needs.

Thousands of curative springs dot the landscape of continental Europe and the British Isles. Like caves, burial mounds, subterranean passages, the shores of lakes, and islands to the west, natural springs are gateways to the Otherworld. Each spring is an orifice—a mouth or vagina—of the mother goddess, a gateway to the realm of the goddess. Though each spring is a repository of the goddess's abundance, the goddess manifests her nature a bit differently in every spring. Like a woman with many attributes to give to life, the attributes conjoined in a single spring are found nowhere else on the surface of the earth.

Natural springs inspired healing and replenishment. Many springs were known to cure barrenness in women, so women went to sleep there, and probably lovers went to the pools together seeking fertility. Some springs in particular were playful meeting places for family and friends, especially in the warm months of summer. Great numbers of pilgrims and relatives prayed at them to propitiate the goddess's favor. The pools near natural springs, particularly thermal springs, also inspired leisure and recreation. When sleeping overnight by the pools, the pilgrims were encouraged to rest and dream the answers to their queries.

In northwest Spain, southern Gaul, and Britain, the spring goddess Coventina was revered, with the height of ritual activity taking place in the late second and early third century, prior to the edict that made such rites illegal in areas under Roman authority. On one stone, Coventina is a nymph, shown resting on waves lapping against a riverbank, waving a water lily playfully in the air with one hand and poising her other arm on an upturned jug of water. At Carrawburgh, along Hadrian's Wall in Northumberland, she is portrayed as a triple nymph. Akin to images of the Triple-Mother Goddess, the face of the three images varies slightly, but her imagery otherwise is standard. She appears semi-nude, pouring a jug of water on the ground with one hand and holding another jug aloft in the other.[97] Over sixteen thousand coins have been found in her well, a level of ritual offerings higher than that at the thermal springs at Aquae Sulis in Bath, England. Other offerings found include jewelry, bits of glass, bone, metal, and leather.[98] Supplicants came to offer prayers and petitions, bathe in the pools, drink from the well, and leave offerings to accompany their prayers.

IF YOU ARE DRAWN TO THIS ORACLE, you want to renew your physical well-being. You may have particular physical ailments. Emotional trauma may also be impairing your health and vitality. You may desire more passion and intimacy in your relationships or in your sexual life. You may be preparing for a life transition requiring greater health and stamina.

The presence of the playful nymph signals the healing of physical distress and the replenishment of vitality. Key to receiving the gifts of her presence is your willingness to receive intimacy and love and to play and frolic. She wants you to have fun, relax, and enjoy life. A healing vacation near water or at a spa may be especially helpful. If you have the opportunity to move to a new home, you might consider living near a river or stream. Professional activities can certainly recede into the background for a while. Perhaps you have been working too hard. Perhaps at this time in your life you need to pause and refresh your physical resources. Perhaps you are approaching retirement, a change in activities or environment, or preparing to give birth to a child. Whatever your situation, this oracle invites you to renew your physical well-being and restore passion, eroticism, and wonder to the physical and sensual activities of daily life.

~ 38 ~
Wells and Thermal Springs

Returning to the Source

Invoking the Qualities of Manifestation and Expression

Wells and thermal springs are natural orifices of the womb of the goddess herself, the warm fires of the earth. Welling up from within, the waters press to the surface of the earth to refresh the land. By tradition, the local king or chieftain mates with the goddess by drinking or bathing in the waters. Fertility for the land is then assured, sometimes by flooding the surrounding land and creating the world anew. This fiery, watery presence of the goddess gives power to manifest inner changes in the outer affairs of life.

It is said that there are some three thousand holy wells in Ireland alone, many abandoned and overgrown, others used only to quench the thirst of livestock, and others engendering pilgrimage and homage throughout the centuries. Often sequestered in lonely hillsides and meadows or nestled in a wooded grove, the ambiance of holy wells is intimate, quieting, and numinous.[99] Now dedicated to St. Brigit, St. Brendan, the Virgin Mary, or one of hundreds of local saints, they were once personifications of mother goddesses, generously welling up water to the surface of the land to sustain life in that locale. At the Well of Doon in County Donegal, for example, the bushes and trees near the well are fashioned with hundreds of rags and torn bits of plastic grocery bags, along with pacifiers, baby ribbons, booties, bibs, trinkets, photos, jewelry, strands of beads, rosaries, crocheted crosses, caps, shoes, and farm boots—all weathering in the wind and rain, the offerings of pilgrims over the years. The well is simple, a level place to kneel and pray and a small, cement-lined pool in which to fill your bottle with water for friends and relatives at home. The prayers for loved ones, for the childless and widowed, for the sick and infirm, and for blessings on family and kin are redolent of memories from an ancient time when wells were the preserves of goddesses and their devoted—though doubtlessly less penitent—supplicants.

In ancient times, people gathered at the goddess's wells for the great solar festivals such as Beltaine (May 1), to celebrate the coming of summer, and Lughnasa (August 1), to celebrate the harvest with ceremony, feasting, games, and races. In modern times, ancient rituals were felicitously attached to saints' days, particularly in midsummer. Most of what we know of these activities comes from eighteenth- and nineteenth-century writers horrified by the "idolatrous" practices of drinking, gambling, and faction fighting occurring on pattern (pilgrimage) days at holy wells.[100]

According to ancient knowing, wells and thermal springs web the landscape with life-giving fertility and generativity. The well opens into the womb of the sacred earth. An overflowing spring is a symbol of robust fertility. A flood destroys and renews the land.[101] The guardian or human protectress of a holy well or thermal spring is female, the few exceptions an overlay, like veneer on an ancient wood. From a set of thermal springs at Bath dedicated to the goddess Sulis, water rushes to the surface at the rate of over a quarter of a million gallons a day. When relaxing or sleeping close to her plenteous waters and steamy breath or luxuriating in her baths, the earth's warmth soothes and refreshes the body. The goddess's presence here is personal, sensuous, and all-embracing.

IF YOU ARE DRAWN TO THIS ORACLE, you want to manifest interior changes in your outer world. You may be feeling even a bit impatient to "get out there" because the vibrancy of your inner life needs exterior expression, affirmation, and contact with others. Your courage and artistry (whether you think of yourself as an artist or not) are urging you to put your dreams and hopes into positive actions and concrete products and activities. Whatever hesitancies you may have, it is time to let them go.

The upwelling of spirit is within you. Like a spring rising to the surface of the land, your creativity is needing expression in the world. No more practicing and preparing to begin. Get going, one step at a time. You must begin by taking the first step, and then another. Don't let seeing the big picture terrorize you, just take the next step toward manifesting your dreams. You already have all the strength and capacity you need. Begin.

~ 39 ~

The Under Tree

Taking Root in the Otherworld

Invoking the Qualities of Exploration and Expansion

While all trees spread upward in the sky, the Under Tree also reaches beneath the ground, extending its trunk and branches within the earth. By following the tree's branches into the earth, the traveler enters the Otherworld beneath the ground. In the Christian period, the Tree of Life grows on the Blessed Isles ever to the west. Forever blossoming and fruitful, the tree supports the maturing of the unseen and unexplored resources in our nature.

A mysterious tree guards the entrance to the Otherworld beneath the ground. By climbing down through its branches, a traveler enters the Otherworld and encounters supernatural figures living there. In the Welsh *Mabinogion*, the legend of "The Lady of the Fountain" tells of the hero Owain, who becomes the champion of the fountain of wisdom and the husband of "the Countess," none other than the sovereign goddess herself.[102] One of Owain's companions, Kynon, tells a story of being directed by the Lord of the Animals to

> *ascend the wooded steep until thou comest to its summit; and there thou wilt find an open space like to a large valley, and in the midst of it a tall tree, whose branches are greener than the greenest pine trees. Under this tree is a fountain, and by the side of the fountain a marble slab, and on the marble slab a silver bowl, attached by a chain of silver, so that it may not be carried away. Take the bowl and throw a bowlful of water upon the slab, and thou wilt hear a mighty peal of thunder, so that thou wilt think that heaven and earth are trembling with its fury. . . . And the shower will be of hailstones; and after the shower, the weather will become fair, but every leaf that was upon the tree will have been carried away by the shower. Then a flight of birds will come and alight upon the tree; and in thine own country thou didst never hear a strain so sweet as that which they will sing.*[103]

The ancient tree is the center of the Celtic world, connecting the earth to the Otherworld below and the sky world above. Its branches reach into the ground and sky. Sometimes the tree is silver and its fruit shimmer like jewels. If an apple tree, a branch from the sacred tree bears blossoms and apples all year long. In the Ulster Cycle, Cú Chulainn's charioteer, Laeg, eloquently describes the ancient tree as he approaches the hallowed realms of the Otherworld:

At the entrance to the enclosure is a tree
From whose branches there comes beautiful and harmonious
music.
It is a tree of silver, which the sun illumines.
It glistens like gold.[104]

IF YOU ARE DRAWN TO THIS ORACLE, the ancient tree beckons you to take root in the Otherworld to stabilize and then expand the hidden and unknown resources of your nature. For centuries, the poets and musicians of the Celtic world have been nourished by otherworldly or spiritual forces within the earth. In this way, poets and prophets break totally new ground, bringing new ideas to awareness. If you accept the invitation, you will begin to explore undeveloped talents and inclinations in your character. Sustained periods of exploration and discovery may be ahead of you. In the Celtic world, the Otherworld is joyous and delightful and never dreary or depressive, so exploring the otherworldly (or inner) side of your nature is likely to be lighthearted and graceful. Supported by an otherworldly merriment, too much work is rarely involved. Rather, the newly matured talents and qualities will add greater depth and dimensionality to your life and work.

~ 40 ~

Chambers in the Earth

Rhythms of the Otherworld

Invoking a Slow and Rhythmical Course of Action

Like their Neolithic and Bronze Age ancestors, the Iron Age Celts use caves and subterranean chambers for shelter, protection, and ritual. On the walls, they carve images of solar wheels and stag hunting, bringing the potency of the sun and the sacred hunt into the earth's interior chambers. These caves and chambers provide refuge from the harsh outer world and connection with the never-ending pulse of life within the earth's sacred interior, the sovereign mother goddess.

In the Valley of Camonica in the Alps of northern Italy, sacred rock carvings enhance the walls of natural caves. Largely composed of solar wheels, stag deer, and hunting scenes, these carvings transport the potency and virility of the sun, the stag, and the sacred hunt into the earth's interior. The rays of sun are depicted as immense antlers spreading like the branches of a tree. Cernunnos, the Lord of the Animals, has antlers flowering out of his head and wears a Celtic torc on each arm. Praying and dancing figures, penises erect, enclose around a stag. A solar figure appears as an arbiter between hunters.[105]

Like many ancient cultures, the Iron Age Celts sought out caves and subterranean chambers for protection and shelter from weather, predators, and enemies. Within them they communicated with the Otherworld and dramatized the bringing and taking of life by depicting the fury of the hunt and the authority of the sun. Within the caves, the natural wombs of the earth, the mysteries of sexual union and fertility could be celebrated in intimate connection with the primal pulse of the sovereign mother goddess, the earth herself.

In later Celtic periods, mythological figures are thought to reside within famous tombs, especially in Ireland. The magnificent megalithic tombs at Newgrange, the Brú na Bóinne, in County Meath, are thought to have been constructed as the abode of the supernatural beings. In Irish literature, Newgrange is the dwelling place of the powerful god Daghdha, his wife, Bóinn, and son, Oengus. The kings of Tara sought to aggrandize their authority by claiming Newgrange and the nearby tombs at Dowth and Knowth as royal burial sites, even in the Christian period.[106]

Hills, mountains, rocks, crevices, and caves are also favored by leprechauns and faeries as dwelling places. As descendants of the people of the goddess Danu, the Tuatha Dé Danann, the faeries have long inhabited the underworld, the subterranean realm just below the ground, living within the ground and especially liking "faery mounds" apart from human habitation. Faeries and leprechauns often slip into the ground invisibly, as if the ground has swallowed them.

IF YOU ARE DRAWN TO THIS ORACLE, the resources and rhythms of nature, and especially the Otherworld, would provide steady continuity in some aspect of your life. Aside from earthquakes affecting the earth's surface, the rhythm or pulse of Mother Earth is largely slow, regular, dependable, and certain. Constancy and consistency bring success.

Your creative ideas and enthusiasm are like the rays of the sun. By stabilizing your ideas and energies in the steady and balanced rhythms common to the earth and the practical aspects of human life, you will complete important projects, build confidence, acquire continuity in relationships, and achieve balance between the creative forces of earth and sky. For now, do not be concerned if you feel that things are going too slowly. Having drawn this oracle, the constant rhythms of Mother Earth are bringing balance and certainty into your life.

Having drawn this oracle, you may feel that a particular quality needs to be solidified to become a more permanent part of your nature. If so, inquire of the oracles once again.

~ 41 ~

Green Man

RENEWAL OF THE EARTH

Invoking Innocence, Easy Progress, and Success

In conveying the fertility of the forest and plants to people and livestock, the Green Man is the consort of the mother goddess, assisting in the greening of spring and summer and the fruitfulness of the earth. The Green Man's face and features are formed of leaves and vines. Deriving his prowess from the earth, he represents the masculine role in sexual coupling, fertility, and the flowering of human life and talent. He signifies innocence, easy progress, and success, especially in initiating new activities.

Throughout Celtic history, mother goddesses have various consorts. Often goddesses and gods, such as Nantosuelta and Sucellus and Rosmerta and Mercury, are consistently paired as divine partners or lovers (see Oracle 15). The Green Man is one such consort, a precociously sexual and youthful consort conveying fertility wherever he goes.

The virility of the antlered god Cernunnos (Oracle 21) and the Green Man are interrelated, so much so that the Green Man might be considered a variant of Cernunnos. From the earliest evidence left by Bronze and Iron Age Celts, Cernunnos presides over the forest, wearing the branching antlers of a stag. His imagery is potent and powerful, assuring the fertility of the natural world in human life. Similarly, in a carving from Germany known as the St. Goar pillar, vegetation grows from the Green Man's head and forms his beard. On the Gundestrup Cauldron, the head of a male is covered with the stylized hair formed of intertwining leaves.[107] As in so many Celtic images the power resides in the head.

Images of the Green Man adorning European cathedrals and churches portray his head and especially his hair, beard, and mustache as a composite of leaves, branches, and vines. Long leaves may stem from his mouth to form an exaggerated beard or mustache. Grapevines, sometimes bearing grapes, run out of the sides of his mouth encircling his head as stylized hair and beard. A mass of leaves may surround his head. His image on the facades and interiors of churches artfully combines the Green Man's foliate persona with figures from the Christian gospels. His appearance is typically placed as though he were an unnamed guardian, as in the Gothic spire of the Münster of Freiburg im Breisgau, Germany. Largely hidden from view from below, heads of the Green Man look down from the open fretwork spire in grief and sorrow at the crucified Christ on the cross below. In a Romanesque carving from Exeter, the Virgin Mary holds her child supported by the foliate head of a Green Man, his eyes closed as though in ageless invocation.[108]

In contrast to the subtle fertility imagery of church art, the explicit, sexual imagery of a youthful consort is boldly portrayed in Irish myth and legend. Like the land itself, Irish legends are rich and moist with youthful sexuality. Much lighthearted phallic humor, for example, quickens the narrative of the Irish epic *Táin Bó Cuailnge* (The Cattle Raid of Cooley). As a responsible sovereign, Queen Medb (often thought to be a personification of a goddess because Celtic tribes did not necessarily have queens) tests the prowess of her many consorts. In their encounter in the wood, Fergus fails to meet Medb's expectations and he "loses his sword."[109] Similarly, Imbolc, the Feast of Brigit celebrated on February 1 (see Oracle 7), is marked with sexual overtones evocative of an older agrarian perspective that linked the fertility of crops, livestock, and humans. According to one folk tradition, the man of the house enters the household in the name of Brigit and "those within . . . go on their knees, open their eyes and admit Brigit," an overtly sexual reference to mating on Imbolc as a means of invoking the blessing of the goddess on the fertility of the household.[110] The robust and fertile image of the Green Man is continued in the Irish Strawboys, the "masked and straw-costumed well-wishers who graced with their presence the house-parties of Irish country weddings."[111]

IF YOU ARE DRAWN TO THIS ORACLE, you are attracting youthful, zestful energy into your life. In the manner of the greening of spring, easy progress is ahead of you. Ideas and actions will seem innocent and spontaneous.

However, your success is limited by natural circumstances beyond your control. Though appearing in many guises through the centuries, the Green Man is always younger and less experienced than the mother goddess, the sovereign Mother Earth. This youthful innocence can accomplish many ends, but you will need greater strength, confidence, and maturity to fully accomplish your goals. By accepting the limits of the situation, you will find much personal satisfaction and ready success. On the other hand, if you overextend your energy or ambition or brashly push ahead, the situation may turn from success to disappointment, and even ridicule.

~ 42 ~

Changeling

EXCHANGE BETWEEN WORLDS

Invoking Otherworldly Knowing and Talent

The Changeling is a faery who has taken the place of a human, often a child or a baby. In more general terms, changelings are people of all ages who bear otherworldly, fey, or faery characteristics, but otherwise live ordinary human lives. Like the Changeling, they may be unusually sensitive and have remarkable talents, such as natural musical abilities, capacity for healing, psychic awareness, or sensitivity to subtle energies. Their exceptional talents become blessings if encouraged and used wisely.

The Changeling is an exchange with the world of the faeries. A faery has taken the place of a friend or neighbor, often a child or a baby. In recent times, these stories have been sinister and frightening, engendering more fear than respect for faery sensitivities and talents. The stories now remaining may be a distorted remnant from a time when an easy and natural exchange between the middle human world and the faery world was commonplace and beneficial.

Throughout the north of Europe, and especially in Ireland, Scotland, and Wales, traditions attest to kidnappings of children by otherworldly beings with sickly or precocious impostors—changelings—left in their place. In Ireland and Scotland, changeling children are sickly, mettlesome, cranky, laugh when misfortune befalls the home, and sometimes have beards and long teeth. Though appearing as children, they typically betray their identity by conversing like adults, revealing ancient knowledge or memory of times long past, rising out of the cradle to play the pipes or the fiddle, or other unnatural actions for a child.[112] Sometimes pipes, a fiddle, or another instrument are left beside the cradle and, when the family hears the most lovely music imaginable, the child is surely known to be a changeling.[113] As many of the Irish and Scottish stories go, the changeling is discovered by a traveling tailor while applying his craft alone with the children:

> *The man of the house wanted some clothes and sent for the tailor to make them. On that day they had a group on the bog cutting turf. Dinnertime came and the woman went out with the food for the men. She told the tailor to mind the babies while she would be out. One of them was at the bottom of the cradle and the other at the top. She wasn't long gone from the house when they spoke in the cradle. "An awkward woman's food for the turf cutters!" said one of them. "Do you remember such and such a war?" said one to the other. "I remember," said he, "and hundreds of wars besides." "Get the violin, Cathal," said the*

other man, "and we'll have a spell of music and dancing." He did and one of them played and the other danced. . . . They warned the tailor not to let on that he knew anything or he would come off worst. When the tailor finishes his work . . . he put a shovel into the good turf fire and "reddened" it twice. . . . When it is red . . . he placed the red shovel under their backsides in the cradle and out the door with them. . . . A woman came to the door, and she threw in one of her own children and after a while, the other one.[114]

Sadly, the belief in changelings has explained childhood diseases and abnormalities and has legitimized the torture of babies in attempts to rid them of the exchange. A unique or exceptional child—or even adult—runs the risk of being thought of as "away with the faeries."

IF YOU ARE DRAWN TO THIS ORACLE, opportunities to encounter or exchange with the Otherworld are possible. There are people of all ages who naturally convey supernatural qualities and often impress others as fey, strange, mysterious, or extraordinary. They often have exceptional supersensory or uncanny abilities, especially in music, healing, or psychic awareness. In drawing this oracle, you may be encountering these otherworldly gifts in yourself or others.

In other ages, knowing things before they occur or at a distance, or healing others through touch and inward knowledge of plants and herbs, was valued and respected. People with such natural talents were recognized early on, encouraged, and trained by elders who had developed and rightfully used these talents. You may now have the opportunity to awaken and develop otherworldly talents in yourself or to support these talents in someone close to you.

~ 43 ~

POOKA

THE TRICKSTER

Invoking the Unexpected, Curious, and Whimsical

A Pooka can turn itself into a horse, a goat, a dog, a cross between a mule, a bullock, and a big black pig, or even a large wool fleece racing about the countryside in the manner of a horse. If an unwary traveler accepts a lift or the Pooka sneaks under and between a man's legs, it may take him for a furious ride atop cliffs and by way of wild and dangerous places. At daybreak, the Pooka tires of the chase and abruptly deposits the rider in a wayward spot. The Pooka is heard chuckling gleefully as it gallops out of sight.

The Pooka is the trickster among the Irish and Welsh goblins and is known to take many forms. Always rough and unkempt, the Pooka appears as a horse, a goat, a dog, or occasionally an eagle the size of a horse. Sometimes the Pooka appears as a ghastly-looking creature resembling a horse with great big long horns or an unknown mix of several animals. Appearing as a horse, it may sneak under a man and between his legs and then take off galloping. At the cave under the Dun of Clopook, there is "a spirit of a Pooka in this cave which frequently [presents] itself in the form of a fleece of wool, which issued from the cave and roamed over the field with astonishing celerity. Its motions were accompanied by a buzzing sound."[115]

Pookas frequently appear around Halloween and May Eve (April 30), when the veil between the supernatural and human worlds grows thin and otherworldly beings and humans may pass more easily to and fro. Occasionally, a kindly Pooka rescues a man or woman from the faery host or other unseen dangers. More typically, though, the trickster Pooka appears to a lost and weary traveler to offer the man a welcome lift home—or somehow manages to get the man on its back. And "when he was on his back, [the Pooka] would race over the tops of cliffs frightening the man riding on him, and when the Pooka was tired of going with him, would bring him back again to the place" where he was before or some lonely spot.[116] The Pooka may laugh heartily as it gallops out of sight. A typical story from County Kerry tells of a saint who was caught out in the woods at night by a Pooka:

> *The saint wasn't long more in the place, when a pooka horse came up to him. The pooka horse told him to come on his back and that he would bring him home. The saint was glad to hear the pooka saying that, and he thanked the pooka and said that he would go up on his back. Anyhow he got up on the pooka's back, and the pooka started running wild around the wood. [He] ran into big heaps of briars and bushes. The poor saint*

couldn't come off his back at all, and the pooka jumped across big glens and big holes and every place worse than another and the saint thought that he would be killed every minute. Anyway the pooka kept going on that way till morning, and he let the saint come off his back when it was bright day.

When the saint was on the ground again, he took a good rest before he started away again because indeed there was a right good fright on him after the night before.[117]

IF YOU ARE DRAWN TO THIS ORACLE, you may expect the unexpected. Tricksters are natural shape-shifters, so the Pooka might show up suddenly in many guises, as unforeseen events, unanticipated circumstances, unique people, or abrupt changes in direction. The Pooka's signaling characteristics are its sudden appearance (as if from nowhere), feeling tricked into doing something you wouldn't ordinarily do (against your better judgment), and perhaps being shaken by a series of seemingly dangerous or reckless events. Despite their unlikely appearance, these unsettling experiences may awaken you to new choices and opportunities. When you least expect it, the Pooka has the pesky habit of picking you up and "dumping" you into new circumstances.

The Pooka is the trickster or prankster of the Celtic world, making mischief with unsuspecting people especially when they feel lost or tired. While the Pooka may frighten and disorient, no one is harmed. Without the Pooka's intervention, you might not have been able to see clearly the circumstances now before you.

~ 44 ~

BANSHEE

THE CALL BETWEEN WORLDS

Invoking Reassurance and Expansion

The banshee's cry announces the threshold between the worlds of life and death. Appearing as a spectral and sometimes beautiful woman, the banshee is a messenger from the Otherworld to this world at the time of death. Coming by night, she is heard shrieking and sobbing outside the family home, at the window of a bedroom, or even seen circling hospitals as death draws near. Favoring families with an "Ó" or a "Mac" in their surnames, banshees lend a curious air of aristocracy to certain Irish families.

Oftentimes among Irish families, death is announced by the unearthly shrieking of the banshee as death draws close. Even the wary among the Irish are more likely to believe in banshees than any other beings of the Otherworld. In *Fairy Legends and Traditions of the South of Ireland*, the memorable words of Thomas Crofton Croker are spoken by the widow MacCarthy lamenting over the death of her son:

'Twas the Banshee's lonely wailing,
Well I knew the voice of death,
On the night wind slowly sailing
O'er the bleak and gloomy heath.[118]

She may be heard or even seen outside the house crying with a lonesome and eerie wail often "all the night through and for three nights after that."[119] The lovely, dainty banshee of the O'Briens wore "white clothes and had a pair of wings."[120] It is said that the banshee heard after the MacCarthys' was "a wild, unkept, [and] haggish creature that seemed in perfect harmony with the dreary and desolate moorland from whence [she] sprang."[121] Banshees are known to lament even over the death of kin who have emigrated to America by circling and shrieking around the family home in Ireland. Like mermaids seen combing their hair on rocks along the coast, banshees are sometimes encountered on a moonlit night combing their long white or golden hair.[122]

For some, the banshee as death messenger is a fearsome, even ghastly creature. If taunted, the trace of her five-finger slap remains indelibly etched upon the cheek. Her shriek can seem to shake a house with terror as if "The cry was dancing on the walls."[123] A fearsome chorus of banshees is still known to wail at battlegrounds where their kinsmen have fallen. More typically, though, banshee stories are respectful and benign, such as this one, which comes from County Wexford in southeast Ireland:

Shortly before my father died. He was dying at the time. Well, he was on his deathbed, we'll say, an' meself an' the woman above, me own woman was up, weren't gone to bed, d'ye know, or anything, an' she was tending to him, an' he—well, he wasn't that bad. He'd live another few days, that kind of a way, d'ye know. But I was sittin' [with] me back to the winda . . . An' did three cries come outside on the cement, on that cement walk, an' I heard them as plain as I can hear meself talking now. . . . An' I didn't say nothin' about it. . . . But I asked 'er after did she hear anythin'? She said she didn't. But I heard three cries outside on the cement. Well, he might live two or three days after that. But that was all.[124]

IF YOU ARE DRAWN TO THIS ORACLE, some aspect of your life or the life of your community is dying. The banshee's call signifies a time when the threshold of the supernatural world draws close. She infrequently comes to the human, Middle World. By fearing death in any aspect of your life, you create needless anxiety. By approaching her generously, her presence brings certainty of the Otherworld. Utterly from another realm, she beckons us across the threshold, encouraging us to see dying aspects of this life as thresholds to an expanded vision.

By looking closely, you will see that death is always near, life and death a seamless passage from one form to another. Draw your attention to the aspect of your question that seeks death and consider the possibilities that beckon from the other side. In this way, by seeing beyond her fearsome aspect, the banshee's call may seem reassuring, even hopeful.

~ 45 ~

Faery Hill

THE HIDDEN WORLD OF FAERIES

Invoking Inspiration

The faeries, the people of the goddess Danu, live as neighbors in the hills and mounds of the countryside. Having yielded the land's surface to the Celts, the faeries now inhabit the Otherworld, beneath the ground, where they live merry and carefree lives. Their supernatural presence brings a lively, nostalgic, and passionate feeling to the landscape, especially enlivening the poetry, music, and song with a sensuous and haunting lyricism. Faery hills, in particular, denote unique sources of inspiration from the faery realms.

With the coming of the Celts to Ireland, the powerful Tuatha Dé Danann, the people of the goddess Danu, eventually retreated from the Middle World on the earth's surface and yielded the land's surface to the Celts. They gently slipped into the Otherworld, where they now live fanciful and merry lives as neighbors in a parallel realm to humans. Living in certain hills throughout the countryside, often ancestral burial mounds called *sidhe* or *sí* (pronounced "shee"), the inhabitants of the *sidhe* are known as faeries. At night some faery hills are seen as ablaze with sparkling lights and alive with merrymaking and music. On certain nights the doors between the worlds open, particularly Samhain (now Halloween), marking the beginning of winter, and May Eve, marking the beginning of summer. On these nights, faeries are often encountered traveling about in our world and may lead humans to gateways to the Otherworld. Familiar caves and cliffs may open, revealing splendid faery castles within. While kindly observers and visitors may be rewarded, interfering with faery hills or castles invites reprisal.

A typical story from Donegal in Ireland tells of a man stacking turf on the bog. Returning at nightfall, he comes upon "a big black hole with mud lying on the surface . . . and a kind of big opening down into the ground. He stuck his stick into it." When he tries to pull the stick out, "what did he do but take a jump into the hole. He went down until he hit hard ground at the bottom and began to walk until he reached a castle where there were many people singing and great entertainment and eating and drinking. He sat in amongst them but he did not eat anything" because he might never return home if he ate or drank.[125]

The presence of the faeries living close by animates the landscape of the earth with lively activity. Along with nature spirits particular to trees, flowers, and features of the landscape, the Otherworld of the faeries imbues the natural, human world with movement, exuberance, and passion. Our world mirrors theirs.

If you are drawn to this oracle, you are attracted to the spiritual forces around you. These spiritual forces, whether faeries or nature spirits, are sometimes the special friends of poets, artists, playwrights, musicians, and the inventive and creative ones of every trade or profession. The presence of the faeries and nature spirits gives the landscape around you its wondrous qualities, and you are attracted to its supernatural qualities.

While the Celts are unusually attentive to the presence of otherworldly beings who share the earth with us, the earth is sacred wherever you live. If you live in nature, especially in secluded places where supernatural beings are more at ease, you may be especially aware of their presence and passionate, spirited vitality. Quite unlike contemporary notions that portray the faeries as fearful and meddlesome, the faeries would much rather cooperate with us, especially sharing inspiration, visions, frivolity, song, and music. Unfortunately, the faeries—and other nature spirits—have become wary of humans, so attracting their support requires respect and care for our natural environment and the spirits who dwell there.

~ 46 ~
Faeries of Mischief and Play

Invoking the Qualities of Laughter, Humor, and Fun

The faeries find humans curiously earnest and somber, and therefore pleasantly amusing. By playing tricks on us, they offset our seriousness with their mischief and humor. They're unusually fond of confounding humans with merry pranks, unexplainable movement and swapping of objects, and fiddlin' merry dance tunes beneath the house. The faeries' presence brings playfulness, frolic, folly, synchronicity, laughter, and fun.

In their own realm in castles beneath the ground, the faeries live lives filled with laughter and merrymaking. Nothing is lacking. Food and drink are plentiful. Their lives are joyous and carefree and without pain, sickness, or suffering. Time seems to be endless and aging is slow, if at all. The faeries are blessed with joy and merriment. Descendants of the goddess Danu, their supernatural qualities supply them plentifully, except for a few missing things that are uniquely of the human Middle World. Two of these are milk and butter, which they steal remorselessly.

Human life seems overly serious and ponderous to the faeries. Humans seem to be in a kind of trance, a stupor in which things seem to be as they appear. So to trick us out of overseriousness, the faeries play pranks on us—traditionally moving the *byre* (the barn) a few paces, stealing objects and leaving something else in its place, swapping a favorite cow and replacing it with an otherworldly cow, conversing with humans from rocks and trees, leaving gold coins about, and playing gay music loud enough to be heard above the ground. The faeries' mischief reveals the "folly of things" and offsets our seriousness with humor and befuddlement. When we take their pranks seriously, they are filled the more with mirth. By following the faeries' mischievous example, human life would seem less ponderous and enlivened with playfulness, laughter, and lots more synchronicity. In a story from Donegal in Ireland, a man gets "magic from the faeries":

> *One fair day he was the only man of the neighbouring townlands who had not a pig to sell. Devil a thing did he do but go into a field and pull a bunch of yellow ragweed and make a pig of it. He went to the fair and his pig was the first sold that day. Well and good. When the buyer was taking the pig home he took it across a place where water was running across the road. Immediately the pig crossed the water [and] it changed into a heap of yellow ragweed. The buyer turned back and made for the fellow and caught him by the shoulders, but the other merely*

swung around in the street and let the arm go with him. The buyer was frightened out of his life and ran off as quickly as he could, but before he went the fellow paid him his money. When the buyer was approaching Killybegs he put his hand in his pocket to see if he had got the right change, and there was nothing there but horse-dung![126]

IF YOU ARE DRAWN TO THIS ORACLE, watch out for fun! Laughter and humor are great medicines. Laughter soothes the spirit and ignites the body with ecstasy. Cutting deftly to the quick, laughing at yourself shatters incrimination and morbid introspection. In strained or new circumstances, humor breaks the ice, because people love to laugh deeply where spirits meet gently, without formalities. Laughter and playfulness have a natural buoyancy that joins easily to joy.

Where is the laughter and fun in your life? How long has it been since you laughed so hard your sides ached? When did you last laugh at yourself? Are you taking anything so seriously that it distorts the fullness of your life? Is the humor of the human condition escaping your notice? The faeries of mischief and humor poke fun at human seriousness so as to bring us more joy. Drawing this oracle suggests that you are approaching the frontier of laughter, merriment, and fun.

~ 47 ~

Faeries of Music, Dance, and the Performing Arts

Invoking Talents and Resources

The faeries are known to love music and dance for a night and a day or even longer. Great musicians, particularly pipers and fiddlers, are inspired by overhearing faery music, happening upon a faery wedding and learning the tunes, or encountering a faery who strokes the strings of a fiddle, forever enchanting it with tunes. So beautiful is faery music that an inspired musician will always be in demand to play and never again be poor.

Legends of music learned from the faeries (and occasionally from mermaids and trolls) are told throughout Ireland and Scotland. By tradition, faery music is the finest music possible, the grandest ever to be heard. As descendants of the Tuatha Dé Danann, the people of the goddess Danu, the faeries are supernaturally inspired with the gifts of music and other creative talents. Faery music, typically encountered on a lovely moonlit night or blown in from the sea, is beautiful and sweet.[127] A human eavesdropper is compelled to listen and join the merriment, and sometimes to dance until rescued, usually a year and a day later.[128]

Great musicians, particularly pipers and fiddlers, and more rarely harpists or fifers, learn their arts from the otherworldly faeries. Often faery celebrations are encountered and faery music is overheard and remembered, or the music is gifted through enchantment and inspiration. A fiddle itself might be magically charmed by a faery, so that it knows every dance tune there ever was. Stories abound, often promoted by the piper or fiddler himself. A great fiddler from Donegal, Neilly Boyle (1891–1960), tells of his night at a faery wedding:[129]

> *Well, I was one night alone with the fairies, and I heard two of the greatest fiddlers ever I heard. They were holding a wedding this night. . . . And, of course, I was introduced to the fiddlers, and I learned a lot from them; never before did I hear such fiddle playing on this world, as I heard them fiddlers play. They played such wonderful embellishments—they said it was the enchanted music of Ireland that was long ago buried, buried since the days of the bards, and the days of the old pipers. But, thanks be to God . . . they bestowed a lot of their knowledge, and . . . I've practiced since a lot of their styles and I have got that secret.*[130]

While most tunes learned from faeries are light and jolly, a well-known Irish slow air called "*Port na bPúcaí*" ("The Faeries' Tune") from the Blasket Islands, County Kerry, is thought to have been overheard by a fiddler. He recalls: "They say [the faeries] are not immortal, they, too, know death, and the music went over the house on the island that night was a lament for one of the faery host that had died and was carried to this island for burial."[131] This tune is nostalgically remembered in a poem, "The Given Note," by Seamus Heaney.

On the most westerly Blasket
In a dry-stone hut
He got this air out of the night.

Strange noises were heard
By others who followed, bits of a tune
Coming in on loud weather

Though nothing like melody.
He blamed their finger and ear
As unpractised, their fiddling easy

For he had gone alone into the island
And brought back the whole thing.
The house throbbed like his full violin.

So whether he calls it spirit music
Or not, I don't care. He took it
Out of the wind off mid-Atlantic.

Still he maintains, from nowhere.
It comes off the bow gravely,
Rephrases itself into the air.[132]

Excelling in the arts, especially in poetry, song, and music, faeries are known to gift humans with special talents and inspiration. A particular faery, known as the Leanán-Sí (pronounced "Lan-awn-Shee") is a special friend to poets. Those inspired by her gifts are thought to live short and brilliant lives.

IF YOU ARE DRAWN TO THIS ORACLE, the spirit world wishes to gift you with talent and creative inspiration. You may even feel as though you have acquired an invisible companion, a kind of muse from the spirit world to guide and inspire you. You may feel gifted by insight or sudden talent, as if inspired from an imperceivable, spiritual source. Music and poetry may seem to be coming out of thin air. If illuminating ideas seem to arise in your mind as easily as air fills your lungs, you are being inspired by the breath of the spirit world.

It is important to be gracious and generous to yourself during special times of inspiration and creativity. For some people, such times can lead to overstimulation and intense activity. Others become drowsy or drift from one thing to another. Still others feel lost or confused. Like prayer and meditation, times of inspiration require personal nurturance and constancy. Be mindful of nourishing yourself with nutritious food, sufficient rest and sleep, healthy exercise, and supportive companionship. By acquiring regular habits of work and relaxation, creative inspiration will become a natural, routine part of your life.

~ 48 ~

Faery Lover

SENSUALITY

Invoking the Qualities of

Pleasure, Delight, and Danger

A faery lover disguises his or her identity and appears as a beautiful man or woman. Approaching by night or in secluded places, the faery lover courts the intended with poetry and song, plays games that delight the senses, or promises riches and happiness as the rewards of marriage. Sometimes a human visits a faery castle beneath the ground and meets a comely lover there. These otherworldly liaisons are short-lived, usually foiled by amiable but cunning trickery.

Passionate love affairs often take place between otherworldly lovers and humans in old Celtic myths. Gods and goddesses seduce human men and woman, usually bringing them back with them into their realms. Children born of these unions are exceptionally beautiful and possess extraordinary powers. In the Irish folk stories, supernatural lovers are typically faeries who come to court and seduce human men and women, especially those who are forlorn or cut off from society.[133] In Scottish tales, the lovers are faeries, selkies, or beautiful seal men from the sea. Always, the lovers are comely and seductive, appearing as human. A selkie lover slips into a lonely man's bed by night to make love tenderly.

In a typical Irish tale, a young orphan girl encounters a handsome faery man while alone: "Day in and day out, she is driven out to mind the cows on every windblown headland and down to Elly Dunes as well. One day she was down there, a young lad came up to her and joined in the conversation with her and when she came home that evening, her stepmother said: 'You must have been playing a lot today, you look terribly worn out.' 'I wasn't doing anything,' says she." The next day and next, she goes out with the cows and each day she fails the more. When finally she confesses the tryst to her stepmother, she advises: "'When he comes to you tomorrow . . . say that there is a very sick calf at home and ask what would cure it.' So the lad told her: 'Tell your mother that hen dung, stale urine, a black-hafted knife and last year's burned palm, all mixed together and sprinkled on the calf, will do the trick.'" Using the magic potion to get rid of the faery man instead, "the stepmother made up a posset and she gave it to the orphan girl." The next day when the girl met the lad, she had the . . . bottle in her pocket. "When the lad sat down beside her, she splashed some of the posset over him. He rose up in a mist and disappeared westwards out over Achill."[134]

The old mythic tales of encounters between Celtic gods and goddesses and human lovers are boldly and playfully erotic. Unlike these ancient stories, tales told in more recent times are sensual and erotic, but rarely directly sexual. Rather than welcomed, otherworldly lovers are typically feared and driven away. Humans rarely visit the faery realms to find lovers there. With passions no longer easily shared between the supernatural world and the human inhabitants of the Middle World, the bold passions of the supernatural realms stay hidden in the Otherworld.

IF YOU ARE DRAWN TO THIS ORACLE, the sensual and sexual side of your nature is wanting attention and care. Your body itself may be wanting deeper and more intimate expression. This oracle suggests that you may be wanting and attracting new (or renewed) relationships that are both loving and fulfilling. Exploring the possibility of a new relationship with your imagination may help to make you more receptive. These new or renewed relationships will bring greater physical and emotional vitality. By being open to new situations (and not repelling them), new acquaintanceships may develop into intimate encounters, friendships, or even partnerships. The faery lover tends to approach quietly and gently, but unexpectedly.

The oracle also suggests that now may be a good time to nourish the normal sensual and sexual needs of the body with comfort, pleasure, and delight. Comforting the body's needs will bring you joy and strength.

Part Four

Oracles of Darkness and Light

Oracles relating to:

Nighttime Stories and Relations

Luminous Spirits of the Night and Death

Beings of Light

Symbols of Light and Rescue

~ 49 ~

NIGHTFALL

THRESHOLDS AND BEGINNINGS

Invoking Interiority and Inner Growth

The Celts favor the night, for darkness renders guidance and mystery. Otherworldly beings quicken, just a little out of sight. Imagine a way of life in which guidance is carved from the stories told and retold in the night and images are born in the long silence of winter. Descending in a hush at twilight, nightfall is the threshold of beginnings. Things newly born are fashioned in the night. Like a womb shielding the land and its people from intrusion, the passage of night gives safe passage to the new.

The early Celts counted time by nights, not by days. The old calendars were oriented more to the cycles of the moon than to the sun. The mysteries of darkness were a protection and a comfort.

At nightfall, after the evening meal, family and neighbors gathered around a single hearth to converse, gossip, and tell tales. Strangers and beggars passing through with news were especially welcome. Stories told in good company in the night had a magic of their own. On special nights, when the mix of song and story was especially inviting, the Otherworld of faeries and ancestors and all manner of nature spirits were present, too, quickening and sometimes humming their own tunes and adding their own stories to the mix.

Night is the time of beginnings, nightfall its threshold. As darkness falls, the veils between the human world and the Otherworld grow thin. Protected as if by a shade, otherworldly dreams, inspirations, whisperings, and reveries are born. Daylight seems too bright for the imagination of the spirit world. Storytelling, inspiration, and creativity require a dimmer light, a gentler light. Things newly born are fashioned in the night. Playing light upon shadow, a flickering oil lamp or fire in the hearth is light enough to spark imagination and the whisperings of the Otherworld. Sometimes even prophesy is born.

In the poem "The Ballad of Father Gilligan," the great William Butler Yeats relays the story of a weary old priest from County Kerry who falls asleep as he prays. As the priest sleeps and another man dies, Yeats describes how the stars—

They slowly into millions grew,
And leaves shook in the wind;
And God covered the world with shade,
And whispered to mankind.[135]

If you are drawn to this oracle, you long to renew your spiritual journey. The time and circumstances are now aligned with moving more deeply into your interior life. You are invited to slow down, quiet down, and deepen your prayer and meditation. By gradually quieting your outer life and the chattering of your mind, you can perceive the inward whisperings of the spirit world. In the Celtic imagination, darkness is a blessing and silence pregnant with possibility. Whether accompanied by others or richly alone to enjoy your nighttime reveries, night is the time for beginnings, insight, and spiritual replenishment. Whether alone or with others, quietude will bring solace and inner joy.

As a womb protects an embryo, the darkness of silence and daily quietude protect and nurture the spiritual life. Like young children, newly born spiritual awareness and insights must be sheltered from harsh probings and questions from the outer world, including your own.

~ 50 ~

Hearth and Family

RIGHT RELATIONS

Invoking Friendship, Family, and Community

Before the advent of electricity, the rural Celts would entertain one another with conversation, riddles, songs, ballads, and storytelling. With a fire brightening and warming a windowless home, a storyteller would blend fact and fiction to form a seamless tale. After working in the fields by day, men and women would gather around a central hearth for evening levity, swapping of news, and storytelling. The mingling of friends and family and the welcoming of strangers around the hearth represent right relations among people.

Alexander Carmichael describes his experience of the evening *ceilidh* (gathering time) of the crofters and farmers of the Outer Hebrides in the late nineteenth century. As evening approaches, the house of the town's storytellers is full, making it "difficult to get inside and away from the cold wind and soft sleet without." The house is

> *roomy and clean, if homely, with its bright peat fire in the middle of the floor. There are many present—men and women, boys and girls. All the women are seated, and most of the men. Girls are crouched between the knees of fathers or brothers or friends, while boys wherever—boylike—they can climb. The houseman is twisting twigs of heather into ropes to hold down thatch, a neighbour crofter is twining quicken roots into cords to tie cows, while another is plaiting bent grass into baskets to hold meal. The housewife is spinning, a daughter is carding. . . . Neighbour wives and neighbour daughters are knitting, sewing, or embroidering. . . . The speaker is eagerly listened to, and is urged to tell more. But, he pleads that he came to hear and not to speak, saying—*
>
> *The first story from the host,*
> *Story till day from the guest.*[136]

The joy and art of ready conversation, music, humor, banter, and repartee are greatly prized in Celtic lands. Even today in Ireland, the soft warmth of a peat fire and lively conversation attract more attention than the nightly news or BBC. In the winter months, much of the home entertainment of Ireland, Scotland, and Wales is graced nightly by the conversation of neighbors, especially if houseguests are willing to oblige an eager audience with tales of distant places (though anywhere will do, like America or England). If you are known for pipin' or fiddlin' or tellin' stories, you will be asked to entertain. A praiseworthy Irish compliment is to be thought a "good crack," that is, capable of setting others laughing, thereby fashioning an atmosphere to forget the cares and struggles of the day. As is proverbial in Ireland, village pubs are the gathering places of neighbors. Here the melodious strains of conversation and music intertwine.

IF YOU ARE DRAWN TO THIS ORACLE, it is time to lighten up on your professional identity and worldly status and cultivate friendship, conversation and camaraderie, and family relationships. This oracle suggests that your life activities have carried you too far adrift from the social activities and ordinary joys of life. Being in right relations with those immediately around you is to be relaxed with the human and unprotected side of who you are. In good company, your identity and attachments to status and worldly pursuits can relax, even if only for a short while. This relaxed demeanor is not the side of your nature that you necessarily take to the office, but the side of your nature that wants to be known and nurtured informally and intimately among those you love and trust.

The art of socializing for the sheer joy of it seems curiously dated in the twentieth century. Nonetheless, all of us need the community of right relations, the cultivation of familiar and relaxed social relationships.

~ 51 ~

Bards

STORYTELLING

Invoking the Qualities of Remembrance and Identity

One local storyteller narrates the history of the people, another relays romantic tales playing fact against fiction, and yet another recites poetry as if words were waves upon the sea. Another storyteller, perhaps an itinerant bard, sings heroic ballads, runes and incantations, songs of romance, or lullabies for children. Genealogies and epics retain the long memory of generations and seldom change. Other stories fashion plots, both old and new, breathing new life and interpretation into changing circumstance.

The most well-known bard of the Celtic tradition is Taliesin Pen Beirdd, the bard of the isle of Britain, who lived in Wales during the second half of the sixth century. A large corpus of songs, poems, and lore are attributed to him. Although much of this work actually comes from medieval times, it is identified with Taliesin to enhance the prestige of the bardic orders in Britain. Nonetheless, the poems of Taliesin stemming from the sixth century, and probably predating his time, relay much of what we know of the ancient bards whose words bestowed blessings on friends and, on the darker side, the curse of satire on foes.[137] Taliesin speaks of his origins:

I was instructor
To the whole universe.
I shall be until the judgement
On the face of the earth. . . .
There is not a marvel in the world
Which I cannot reveal.[138]

Notwithstanding Taliesin's immodesty, the bards conveyed through the centuries the mysteries of lore and tradition. Stretching back before recorded time, the most important role of itinerant bards and village storytellers was to preserve a vast body of oral lore, including history and genealogies, poems and songs, epic tales, riddles, incantations, knowledge of disputes and settlements, and law.

Traveling from parish to parish in the late nineteenth century, Alexander Carmichael visited many such storytellers and recorded their tales and songs. The storytellers Carmichael sought out were already old; they had learned their poems and stories as children from old storytellers who had learned them when they were children. In this manner, the tales and poems Carmichael collected travel back in memory to the first half of the seventeenth century.[139] Carmichael tells of an itinerant storyteller of early eighteenth-century Scotland, one Catherine Macaulay, who "wandered from house to house, and from townland to townland . . . and remained in each place longer or shorter according to the population and the season. . . . [reciting] night after night, and week after week . . . poems and stories . . . long and weird."[140] One storyteller of the Outer Hebrides was Janet Campbell, a nurse, who "had many beautiful songs and lullabies of the nursery. . . . [H]er stories had a charm for children . . . listening to what the bear said to the bee, the fox to the lamb, the harrier to the hen, the serpent to the pipet, the whale to the herring, and the brown otter of the stream to the silvery grilse of the current."[141]

IF YOU ARE DRAWN TO THIS ORACLE, knowing and interpreting the long story of your life—or the long story of your family, community, or people—is important to you. Sacred texts, great literature, or science fiction that probes the boundaries of the future may unexpectedly seem more relevant to you.

Some of your own life stories will not change, or only slightly. Others, reflected in the mirror of current circumstance, will change dramatically. In the act of telling stories, the past more consciously bears upon the present. Former times are revisited and integrated, sometimes in startling ways. Familiar and seemingly stray events are probed for meaning. In your stories, the familiar and unusual are bound to mingle, forming the rich contours and patterns of your life.

The art of storytelling is active, not passive. Though a story is unchanged from an earlier telling, it nonetheless brings reminiscence, meaning, and identity. What is more, a changing story may contain the promptings and guidance of spirit. Watch your own tellings for changes—they may indicate a shifting of awareness as well as prospects for the future.

~ 52 ~

Presence of Ancestors

THE ANCIENT ONES

Invoking the Sanction and Good Fortune of Ancestors

For the tribal Celts, ancestors were as lively as the living, as mingling lights and shadows cast upon the hills. Ancestral burial mounds were revered by successive generations, for they preserved the authority of the ancestors and yielded access to the Otherworld. The Celts solicited guidance, protection, and favor from ancestors who were particularly alert to their individual, family, and tribal needs. Honoring the ancestors signified the continuing good fortune of past generations.

Ancestral burial mounds were the center of ritual activity for tribal Celts. The good fortune of ancestors was signified by the very existence of the tribe. If ill fortune, such as famine or pestilence, had overcome them, the tribe would have vanished from the land. Soliciting the favor of past generations brought the prosperity of the ancestors to the present generation and hopefully to generations yet to come. As modern-day Catholics solicit the favor of saints, invoking the ancestors (or particular ancestors) rendered their lively presence in the mundane affairs of life. The tribal community was naturally aligned with and nurtured by the presence of their ancestral burial grounds.

Before the coming of Christianity to Ireland in the fourth and fifth centuries, the land was divided into many land holdings called *tuaths* ruled by local chieftains. Each *tuath* had an ancestral burial mound, often surrounded by an earthen wall called a "ring fort" marking its circumference.[142] In Scotland, the land was similarly controlled by clans and their chieftains. Since a people's vitality and prosperity were aligned with the land itself and her ancestors, it was dangerous to migrate and inauspicious to travel. The literal dangers of traveling notwithstanding, departing from the protection of one's ancestors courted misfortune, as attested by Alexander Carmichael's many renderings of plaintive blessings for traveling sons and daughters among the country people of the Outer Hebrides, even as late as the nineteenth century.

In the *Carmina Gadelica*, Alexander Carmichael recorded the observances and festivals surrounding the festival of St. Michael the Victorious, the most imposing pageant demonstration of the Celtic year in the western coasts and isles of Scotland. The activities involve hymns celebrating fertility, lovemaking, and the giving of love-gifts praising progeny and prosperity. Special cakes called *struan* were made for both the living, the absent, and the dead. On September 29, the day of the festival, the people of the various villages set out on horseback to make their pilgrimage circuit of St. Michael's burial ground.

On reaching their destination . . . And commending themselves and their horses to the leading of the valiant, glorious archangel of the cornered shield and flaming sword, the people remount their horses to make . . . the circuiting of the burial ground. The great crowd starts from the east and follows the course of the sun in the name of God, in the name of Christ, in the name of Spirit. . . . At the end of the circuit the "culag" *[the young maiden] gives to her* "bialag" *[young man] . . . a handful of carrots, saying—*
Progeny and prosperity on thy lying and rising.[143]

IF YOU ARE DRAWN TO THIS ORACLE, your ancestors are wishing to support and accompany your actions. Regardless of what you might think of their actions when they were alive, they survived to give progeny, and their good fortune and favor are a part of your inheritance. In former times, when the attention to ancestors was cultivated and the veils between life and death seemed thinner, it was quite possible to feel much akin to those you had never met.

Now is a fine time to explore your ancestral roots or your extended family. You may find unexpected links in your personality and life history with those who have gone before you. You may wish to chart your genealogy, reconnect with members of your extended family, or visit the homeland of your ancestors.

Having drawn this particular oracle, one (or several) of your ancestors may wish to guide you and forward your well-being. You might feel that some invisible presence is accompanying you and pointing the way. An approaching danger may suddenly veer off course and pass you by. New stories may unexpectedly enter the storytelling life of your community, family, or your own life tale, adding new elements to a well-known tale. Your intuition may seem unusually alert, highlighting the colors and circumstances around you and making them crystal clear, distinguishable, and memorable. Guidance comes in many forms. Be alert.

~ 53 ~

NEW MOON

WISDOMS OF THE HEART

Invoking Tenderness and Compassionate Knowing

According to the old traditions, the moon is revered as the queen of the night, beauteous and fair. On seeing the new moon rising in the night, the men and women of old Scotland and Ireland bow gently, bending a knee in admiration. "Hail to thee, thou new moon, guiding jewel of gentleness!"[144] Shining in the night sky as the queen maiden of guidance and good fortune, the new moon brings graciousness and maidenly joys to daily life. She signifies tenderness, compassion, and the intelligence of a loving heart.

Along with reverence and rites concerning the sun, stars, and fire, lunar worship is a common feature of the old ways of the Celtic people. Alexander Carmichael, recording the prayers and customs of the Scottish Highlands and the Outer Hebrides in the late nineteenth century, observed these vanishing customs and rites, still then extant among the country people.

In the Island of Barra of the Outer Hebrides, the old men and women "make obeisance to [the new moon] as to a great chief. The women curtsy gracefully and men bow low, raising their bonnets reverently. The bow of the men is peculiar, partaking somewhat of a curtsy of the women, the left knee being bent and the right drawn forward towards the middle of the left leg in a curious but not inelegant manner."[145] Carmichael records several invocations and prayers hailing the new moon, the jewel of the night sky:

Hail to thee, thou new moon,
Guiding jewel of gentleness!
I am bending to thee my knee,
I am offering thee my love.

I am bending to thee my knee,
I am giving thee my hand,
I am lifting to thee mine eye,
O new moon of the seasons.

Hail to thee, thou new moon,
Joyful maiden of my love!
Hail to thee, thou new moon,
Joyful maiden of the graces!

Thou art travelling in thy course,
Thou art steering the full tides;
Thou art illuming to us thy face,
O new moon of the seasons.

Thou queen-maiden of guidance,
Thou queen-maiden of good fortune,
Thou queen-maiden my beloved,
Thou new moon of the seasons![146]

IF YOU ARE DRAWN TO THIS ORACLE, you are learning to see with the eye of the heart. There are meanings, understandings, and discernments known to the heart alone, and rarely seen or understood by the intellect, the discriminating mind.

When you begin to see with the eye of the heart, it will be as though a veil has been lifted before you. You will see more deeply into the nature of things, relationships, and events. Your discriminating mind will relax. With your actions more in accord with natural patterns around you, you will interfere less, allowing others and events to mature according to their own design and necessity. Your actions will be more secure and compassionate, supportive of what is implicitly good and natural. In time, these softer wisdoms of the heart will bring you greater wisdom and nobility of character.

~ 54 ~

Esus Cutting the Tree

SACRIFICE

Invoking Surrender of the Old and Receptivity to the New

The unique image of Esus portrays him as a woodcutter chopping down a tree. The young woodcutter, the surrounding animal and bird imagery, and the prominence of the tree as a symbol of life all hint at a once popular myth. Throughout the Celtic world, trees were (and still are) considered sacred, and indiscriminately cutting one down was punishable by tribal law. To sacrifice a tree signifies the relinquishing of the familiar for the new and unknown.

The complex and evocative imagery of two stone bas-reliefs from the first century portray a young man chopping down a tree or cutting branches off a tree, surrounded by the imagery of a bull and three cranes or egrets. The larger of the two monuments, discovered in 1711 at the site of Notre Dame in Paris, is dedicated to Jupiter during the reign of Tiberius by a guild of sailors, and consists of six beautifully carved stones. On one stone is a large bull standing in front of a willow with two cranes on his back and a third perched on his head. On an adjoining stone, a woodcutter chops at the branches of a willow. Inscribed above the bull and waterbirds is *Tarvostrigaranus*, meaning "The Bull with Three Cranes," and the woodcutter Esus, meaning Lord. The other, more dramatic stone monument from Trier, Germany, combines these images, evoking the drama of a complex myth of which we know little aside from the images and inscriptions themselves. On the stone from Trier, a woodcutter chops at a willow surrounded by the head of a bull and three cranes or egrets.[147,148]

A woodcutter and willow so artfully depicted evokes the portrayal of a sacred act, probably ritually enacted. The bull signifies the powers of the Otherworld, especially potency. The waterbirds connect the image to lakes and marshes, thresholds of the Otherworld. The graceful willow is native to the banks of rivers and lakes and especially prevalent in marshes. All trees are sacred, symbolizing the passage of life and death in its cycle of growth. In temperate climates where deciduous trees so noticeably change with the season, this symbolic Tree of Life dramatizes the passage of life each year. As seen in the tree oracles (Oracles 25–28) and especially regarding the thorn tree, the violation of such a tree brought havoc to human life and was often punishable by tribal law. To cut or chop a tree signifies a ritual act of sacrifice and surrender to the numinous forces that impinge every day on human life, an awareness perhaps unsettling but always familiar to the rural and agrarian Celts, and other indigenous cultures worldwide.

If you are drawn to this oracle, your deep instincts are pulling you into new endeavors and prospects and away from the known and familiar. Now is a great time to sacrifice graciously the old for the new. The new needs space in which to grow. By voluntarily clearing your life of the clutter of unnecessary habits and possessions, the transition will be much easier. If you can just clear your thoughts, fresh thoughts and ideas are ready to arise in your imagination. Your dreams and daydreams are probably already guiding you. Little can stop you except your own holding on to well-known habits and patterns of the past.

It may be important to do some practical things, such as cleaning your house, closets, garage, attic, basement, office, studio, or desk to initiate clearing your life of the useless debris that invariably accumulates. Throw away or store out of sight things you are no longer using. Then rest and wait for your imagination to awaken and your new life to begin.

~ 55 ~

Hammer God

SCEPTER OF AUTHORITY AND CHOICE

Invoking the Qualities of Wise and Just Decisions

The Hammer God is primarily a tribal father god, wielding his hammer or mallet as a symbol of authority and command. Of mature age and kindly disposition, he is the most good-natured and benevolent of the major male deities. Frequently holding a pot or goblet or standing near wine barrels, he is also linked with the inexhaustible cauldron of the Otherworld. His Celtic name is Sucellus, meaning "The Good Striker," and his presence brings wise and judicious decision making, especially in community affairs.

The Hammer God had widespread influence throughout the Rhineland and ancient Gaul, extending southward to the mouth of the Rhone. Over two hundred stone and bronze representations have been found, largely along the Rhine and the Rhone River valleys. His mature and kind appearance lends a benign and fatherly presence. In the image on page 190, he not only carries a large club but his erect penis depicts power and robust fertility. He holds a hammer or mallet, his signature attribute among many Celtic tribes. Often the hammer is crudely carved; sometimes it is realistically portrayed, with a long-shafted handle and metal blade. Occasionally, a double-ax, suggestive of unlimited authority, is present along with the hammer. The Hammer God is so ubiquitously associated with the hammer that sometimes his presence is marked by the symbol of the hammer alone.[149]

The most prominent father-god of Irish mythology is the Daghdha, meaning "the good god." He is one of the Tuatha Dé Danann, the people of the goddess Danu. Like the Hammer God, he wields an enormous club, suggestive of authority, fertility, and perhaps its role as an agent of renewal. Another of the Daghdha's attributes is his possession of an enormous, inexhaustible cauldron, also associated with the otherworldly powers of the mother goddesses.[150]

In a similar manner, the Gaulish and Rhineland Hammer God is also associated with pots, goblets, and wine barrels, particularly in wine-producing regions like Burgundy. Though always signified as holding a hammer or mallet over one of his shoulders, he sometimes carries a pot or goblet as well, or stands with wine barrels at his feet.[151] This association assumes his protection of the grape harvest and the production of wine.

If you are drawn to this oracle, you need to make wise and careful decisions regarding your own resources and activities, and perhaps those affecting a large number of people, such as your extended family or community. Others are looking to you for guidance, leadership, and support.

You must consider the situation perspicaciously, carefully examining the circumstances and options, as well as the possible outcomes of your present actions. You may need to be very patient, waiting for information to form a discernible pattern. Only then can you make prudent decisions. The fatherly presence of the Hammer God signals an auspicious opportunity to better your own circumstances and the circumstances of those for whom you are responsible. If you take sufficient time and care to listen to all sides of the discussion and weigh all the possible outcomes, you will not only be successful but garner the esteem of your family and community.

~ 56 ~

HEAD

IMMORTALITY

Invoking the Refinement of Character

The sublimity of the human head is reflected in the Celtic stories and iconography, for the head conveyed the essence of a person and lived beyond the life of the body. Celtic warriors collected the heads of battle victims, hanging them from their belts or setting them apart on stones. Bran the Blessed instructed his companions to bury his head facing east on White Mount in London to guard Britain from invasion. The exaggerated Celtic head signifies the continuity and immortality of each human being.

In their artwork, the Celts frequently exaggerated the size of the human head and portrayed facial features, hair, and expression in the eyes with consistently finer detail than given to other parts of the human body. A large head might be expertly carved, with little attention given to the rest of the body and with limbs appearing diminutive by comparison.[152] The large size and refined detail of the head give the image a lively, immediate, and personal character. Even apart from accompanying symbols, one senses that the expression alone relays identity and, by inference, an epic tale or heroic account.

Greek and Roman writers were ready to criticize the much-feared Celts and inform us that they practiced head-hunting, decapitating the victims of war and keeping the heads as trophies or offering them in shrines dedicated to the purpose. In southern Gaul at Roquepertuse, a shrine-portico from the second century was arrayed with niches containing skulls of young men who had died in battle. Epics from ancient Ireland and Wales portrayed warriors collecting the heads of battle victims.[153] Even into the nineteenth century, the heads of Christian saints were thought to endow wells with holiness and healing powers and the heads of evil people to poison a well.

The well-known tale of Bran the Blessed (Bendigeidfran) from the Welsh *Mabinogion* is a fine example of the divine properties thought to be encapsulated in the head. Bran was of supernormal size and of the royal family ap Llyr of Harlech in Wales. His sister Branwen was married to the king of Ireland, who, upon returning with her to Ireland, treated her as a servant. In time, Branwen trained a young starling to speak and sent it across to Wales to relay her plight to Bran, who immediately mobilized his armies against Ireland. Bran's forces won, but only seven warriors survived, and Bran himself was fatally wounded in the heel by a poisoned spear. Bran then summarily commanded his men:

> *"And take the head and carry it to Gwynfryn [White Mount] in London," said Bendigeidfran, "and bury it with its face toward*

France. You will be on the road for a long time: you will be feasting in Harlech for seven years with the birds of Rhiannon singing to you, and the head will be as good company for you as it ever was when it was on me. Then you will be in Gwales in Pembroke eighty years, and until you open the door toward Aber Henfelen . . . you can remain there, and the head untainted, will be with you. But from the time you open the door you cannot remain there, go to London and bury the head. . . . Then his head was struck off, and the seven men and Branwen as the eighth began the crossing.[154]

IF YOU ARE DRAWN TO THIS ORACLE, you are invited to refine your character. Your character will outlast the death of your physical body. In the Celtic imagination, the refinement or coarseness of your character continues after death. The head of a person even converses with companions and endows wells and shrines with personal properties. Most religious traditions worldwide aver the continuity from life to death in some form, whether it be immortality, reincarnation, or the memories of future generations. Even if you do not personally believe in a form of life after death, considering what you leave to future generations after your death will give maturity and perspective to your daily activities.

Having drawn this oracle does *not* suggest that death is close, but that your present circumstances give you a unique opportunity to focus on refining your character. You are urged to look carefully at the people and challenges in your life that invite greater subtlety and nobility.

~ 57 ~

Sun God

GOD OF THE SKY

Invoking the Qualities of Power and Radiance

The power of the sun to give light and warmth and its return each day have been revered for thousands of years, from the time of the Bronze and Iron Age Celts. Portrayed as a spoked wheel or swastika, the sun rolls across the firmament pulled by a chariot and team of horses. Among the romanized Celts, a powerful sky god brandishes his solar wheel as a shield as he crushes the head of a monster with his foot or hand. The sun god signifies majesty, power, radiance, fertility, and beauty.

The sun gives warmth, light, and cycles to the year and is therefore associated with the giving of life, fertility of the crops, and the conquering of menacing forces. Complementary to the earth's primal power over life, the sun touches the earth and sparks the life already there. From archaeological evidence from the Bronze and Iron Age through the mythological period, the allusion to sexual coupling is obvious: the warmth of the sun enters the moist interior of the earth where life begins. Solar images adorn the bodies and are conveyed by goddesses and gods alike. In the Camonica Valley in northern Italy, the Celts of the late Bronze and Iron Age carved on cave walls solar images, round disks or spoked wheels held aloft or volleyed by human figures.[155] The Gundestrup Cauldron bears the image of a magnificent sky god portrayed as being upheld, perhaps conveyed, by a wheel. Small clay figures of young goddesses are affixed with sun wheels surrounding their bodies or adorning their breasts, bellies, and thighs.[156] Images of the sun and earthly abundance appear to harmonize in the Celtic imagination. Though sun images are primarily associated with male deities and images of earthly abundance with mother goddesses, it is not uncommon to find goddesses associated with sun wheels and gods carrying cornucopiae and signs of a prosperous harvest.

Images of the sun wheel and swastikas, sometimes accompanied by a chariot and horse, on cave walls, coins, and armor, distill in imagery the mythic portrayal of the sun conveyed across the sky by a chariot and a team of horses. Perhaps only an animal as prestigious as a horse could accompany the sun. Epona, the horse goddess, is sometimes accompanied by solar imagery.[157]

Solar deities in the Roman period, however, became increasingly masculine and fierce, though benevolent toward those they protected. Borrowing some of Jupiter's appearance from the Romans, the Celtic Jupiter is a powerful god, portrayed as standing and holding his solar wheel authoritatively. He frequently appears as a victor and as a god of generous mien and majesty, mounted on a horse and brandishing his (entirely Celtic) solar wheel like a shield against the enemy. Beneath him, pressed down by his foot or hand, is a monstrous, serpentlike creature. The Celtic Jupiter is a warrior god, conquering the hideous forces troubling human life.[158]

Two of the great fire festivals of the Celtic world, Beltaine at the coming of summer (May 1) and Lughnasa at the coming of the harvest (August 1), ritualize fire as the sun's semblance on earth. The cycles of the sun bring life. Celebrated into the nineteenth century, a midsummer celebration in Germany, for example, involved setting a wheel of straw on fire and rolling it down a mountain into the Moselle River. If the wheel reached the river still ablaze, a good wine harvest was foreseen.[159] Similarly, the great fire festival of the Christian year, Easter, became associated in time with the sun. On Easter, the country people in Ireland rose early in the morning in hopes of seeing the "sun dancin' in the sky."[160]

IF YOU ARE DRAWN TO THIS ORACLE, you are sensing a fiery power emanating toward you or from within you. You marvel at the majesty of the sky world and the delicate fabric of life stirred by sunlight. You cannot seem to get enough sunlight. The brilliance of light attracts you. You may want to wear bright jewelry, or even be attracted to precious gems, especially diamonds.

Drawing this oracle suggests that you have an opportunity to attract majesty and radiance to your character and attitude toward life. This is your time in the sun, a time to shine, bringing a sparkling quality to your own life as well as to others'. If you are attracted to a spiritual path, you may sense an inner light that propels you to focus more intensely on your meditations, prayers, or practices toward gaining enlightenment.

The sun's constancy and radiance invariably help to instill confidence and assurance. Positioning your life within the sun's beneficence brings balance to the flow of ordinary life events. In sensing the constancy of movement beneath change, hard times will bestow resilient and bountiful times, steadiness, and hope. By mindfully drawing closer to the sun's radiance, your life will seem more buoyant, majestic, powerful, and inspiring.

~ 58 ~

TARANIS

GOD OF LIGHTNING AND THUNDER

Invoking Action and Vigilance

Taranis is the Celtic thunderer, his name derived from the Celtic word for thunder, *taran*. A sky god associated with the heavens and storm clouds, Taranis presides over the weather and conditions of men and women below. The flash of lightning and the roar of thunder signify the capricious nature of the elements and the fortunes of human life. Often allied with the sky god Jupiter, Taranis brings a thunderous, mercurial temperament and destructive character to the company of sky deities.

Little is known about Taranis, the god of lightning and thunder. The archaeological evidence is scarce, with merely seven altar dedications to Taranis among the Roman-Celtic areas of Britain, Gaul, the Rhineland, and Dalmatia (former Yugoslavia).[161] It is possible that dedications on statuary of Taranis may have been rough-hewn and, like Taranis himself, exposed to the elements, perhaps placed in locations adjoining mountaintops where lightning and thunder were likely. He is closely associated with Jupiter, the most prominent of the sky deities.

Infrequent allusions to Taranis by Roman writers, such as the poet Lucan, are so unflattering that it is improbable that they are impartial, but rather made by a citified outsider commenting about the customs of the rural and agrarian Celts. Lucan, in his *Pharsalia*, avers that the Gauls encountered by Caesar's army witnessed the making of offerings, blood sacrifices, and even human sacrifices to the shadowy gods Taranis, Teutates, and Esus, though little else is said of them.[162]

As the god of thunder and lightning, Taranis can convey destruction and chaos among his wary supplicants.

IF YOU ARE DRAWN TO THIS ORACLE, your life probably feels beset with unforeseen changes. The swift pace of events can be unnerving and confusing. This oracle suggests that events are set into motion by natural forces outside your control. You are cautioned to be careful about your speech and actions and yet to be ready to act swiftly, especially if you or others are in danger.

Taranis is associated with the forces of nature. As it is prudent to take precautions and go indoors in inclement weather, it is wise to act in a restrained manner and to maintain a low profile when the circumstances of your life are shifting rapidly. Strategizing is often useless, even unwise, not only because of changing circumstances, but also because your mental clarity may be impaired. Like changes in the weather, the fast pace now occurring in your life will change soon. This oracle cautions against undue anxiety and suggests combining restraint and readiness in your present actions.

~ 59 ~
Oengus/Mabon
YOUTHFUL CHAMPION, SON OF LIGHT

Invoking the Defense of Innocence, Love, and Virtue

Oengus is the son of a secret union of Daghdha, the Good God, and Bóinn, the river goddess. Oengus sees a girl in a dream and falls in love with her. Though he finds her and her companions living in a lake, they are shape-shifters who transform into swans every other year. Unable to persuade the girl's father to allow him to wed her, he turns himself into a swan and they fly away together as swans. Oengus represents heroic love, innocence, virtue, and the overcoming of obstacles.

In Irish myth, Oengus is the heroic champion. Variously known as the son of the goddess or the son of light, Oengus is one of the Tuatha Dé Danann, a race of supernatural beings forced to dwell underground with the coming of the Celts to Ireland. In the mating of the river goddess, Bóinn, and the Good God, Daghdha, Oengus is conceived. In order to hide their secret union, Bóinn and Daghdha cause the sun to stand still in the heavens for nine months, giving the appearance that Oengus is conceived and born on the same day. Imbued with the armor of the sun, Oengus becomes a wondrous youth, the champion of love, innocence, and virtue.

As a young man, Oengus dreams of a young girl he does not know. Upon awakening, he is passionately in love with her and sets out searching the countryside to find her. When at last he finds Caer ("Yew Berry"), she is living in a lake, a portal to the Otherworld. Caer and her girl companions are shape-shifters, and every other year, at the festival of Samhain, they turn into swans. All of them have lovely chains around their necks, except Caer's is made of gold. Though Oengus begs to marry Caer, her marriage signals the father's death and he adamantly refuses. Only at Samhain, when the thresholds between the worlds are as thin as veils, might he escape with her. Waiting until Samhain, Oengus turns himself into a swan and he and Caer fly away together, circling the lake three times to enchant the inhabitants to sleep for three nights and three days.[163]

In the Welsh tradition, the youthful champion is the son of the Modron, the mother goddess. He is called Mabon, taken from his mother at the age of three days and held captive in a prison by Arthur for uncounted centuries. When, countless ages later, he is released, Mabon is older than any living creature. Of supernatural birth, he is destined to be a champion of the right and those on quest for the sake of love: Mabon's assistance allows Arthur and Culhwch to overtake Twrch Trwyth, a fierce wild boar, and to seize the scissors, razor, and comb between its ears. It is a quest within a quest, and only by securing this extraordinary prize can Culhwch wed Olwen, the object of his impassioned love.[164]

Born of supernatural origins, Oengus and Mabon are prefigured champions, each a wondrous child (see Oracle 16), who has grown older to overcome the impossible.

IF YOU ARE DRAWN TO THIS ORACLE, you are a champion of unpopular causes. You want to live honorably and honestly even if it costs you time and money. Pursuing honest work and maintaining faithful relationships are extremely important to you. Male or female, you are developing the noble character of a knight, striving from a sense of fidelity and virtue on behalf of everyone. In this matter, you are capable of great accomplishments, overcoming obstacles that would seem hopeless and fearful to most people.

Having drawn this oracle, you may also be facing a situation that tempts you away from virtuous actions and toward an easier and more convenient course. Do not mistake expediency for virtue. As with champions, you are being tested. Look closely at the situation, seeking to see the good, innocent, reliable, and honest. Any gain from acting cheaply or deceitfully will be temporary and vacuous. Rather than acting imprudently, act from a sense of principle. Whatever your age, the oracle promises you a youthful energy to champion an honorable cause, action, and outcome.

~ 60 ~

Lugh/Lludd

Warrior, The Shining One

Invoking the Quality of Mastery

The Irish warrior Lugh is the master of all the arts. When he approaches Tara, the fort of King Nuada, the king's eyes are dazzled by the bright light of Lugh's countenance, as though he has gazed straight into the sun. Lugh's counterpart in the Welsh tradition is the warrior-king Lludd, who joins with his brother Llewelys to overcome the three plagues oppressing the Isle of Britain. A warrior's special quality is mastery of all the arts, including poetry, music, smithing, pageantry, and healing.

Long ago in Ireland, in mythological time before the time of the Celts, the Fomorians lay siege on the Tuatha Dé Danaan, who were living peacefully on the emerald isle. Among them, Lugh is a warrior more beautiful and noble than any man. Born of supernatural origins, he is the son of a prince of the Tuatha Dé and a Fomorian princess, the grandson of the powerful Fomorian king, Balor of the Evil Eye. When Lugh approaches the gates of Tara accompanied by his warriors, he gains access to the king's court as the master of all the arts, including carpentry, smithing, music, combat and war, poetry, magic, healing, cupbearing, pageantry, and gaming. Once the Tuatha Dé king, Nuada, sees that Lugh is matchless in all the arts, he enlists his aid against Balor. Soon, Lugh enlists the help of Manannán Mac Lir, the powerful ruler of the sea. From Manannán, he acquires a breastplate that no weapon can pierce and a sword whose thrust no one can survive. As Nuada watches Lugh and his warriors returning to Tara, his

> *eyes were dazzled by a bright light as if he had looked full into the sun, but then he saw the brilliant rays shone from the face of the leader of the troop and from his long golden hair. Darts of light came off the young man's armour and off his weapons and the gold-embossed harness of his horse. A great jewel blazed from the front of the golden helmet he wore on his shining hair, and Nuada knew that Lugh had come back to Tara.*[165]

As soon as Lugh takes his seat in the court of the king, a horde of slovenly Fomorians bears down upon Tara. To Lugh's horror, when the unkempt men stumble into the court, Nuada and his household rise to their feet. When Lugh protests, Nuada replies that these Fomorians are returning to claim their taxes and a third of the crops and a third of the children as slaves. Outraged, Lugh brandishes Manannán's sword and kills all but nine of the Fomorians, sparing them only to turn to Balor with Lugh's deadly reply.[166]

The Tuatha Dé Danaan and the Fomorians prepare for war. King Balor, Queen Ceithlinn of the Crooked Teeth, their twelve sons, and a great army of warriors march across Ireland to Tara. On the Plain of Moytura, the ground becomes "slippery with blood" as men fight and die, friend and foe side by side. When Balor fells Nuada with a single blow, Lugh is so enraged that he taunts his grandfather Balor to lift the eyelid of his deadly eye. Ten Fomorian warriors pull on ropes, as though drawing a curtain, to raise the weighty lid. Lugh thrusts a stone from his sling into Balor's eye as it opens, killing him instantly as the eye falls back through Balor's head. Though the dead are "as countless as flakes of snow," the Fomorians are forever routed from Ireland.[167]

IF YOU ARE DRAWN TO THIS ORACLE, you are attracting adventure and challenges to your life. This oracle signifies the actions of a mature and seasoned warrior, capable in many arts of action and contemplation. Seasoned warriors do not go out looking for high adventure, but challenges seem to find them nonetheless. To meet approaching events, you will want to combine authority with grace, skill, and artfulness. In acquiring many skills, you will be both flexible and strong. A true warrior has complete command of her or his actions. By coupling your skills to one another in your actions, you will master both the situation and yourself.

If the present situation is dangerous to yourself or others, wise action is to seek guidance and assistance. A warrior rarely journeys alone, but is accompanied by kindred companions and trusted friends or advisors. Pursuing worthy and risky objectives without the aid and wise counsel of others is unwise and sometimes perilous. Concerted action adds strength to strength.

~ 61 ~

Charioteer/The Chariot

RESCUE FROM DANGER

Invoking the Qualities of Trustworthiness and Loyalty

A chariot and team of horses pull the sun across the sky. In the blessed isles, golden chariots seem to rise "with the tide towards the sun."[168] The charioteer's art is to stand loyal to the champion in the heat of battle. Withdrawing the war chariot slightly apart from the fray, the charioteer stands ready to rescue the champion if the battle presses too dangerously. The charioteer's qualities are intense personal loyalty and trustworthiness, especially amid the fervor of turmoil and change.

The Celts were terrifying fighters, much feared by the Romans. Combining the swift movements of the calvary with two-wheeled war chariots, the chariots raced between the lines and harassed the enemy. The screaming of instruments, the howling of warriors, the rattle of chariot wheels, the neighing of horses, and the confusion were ghastly. Darting back and forth between the lines of comrade and foe, each chariot carried a warrior, charioteer, and weapons behind well-trained horses. Julius Caesar in *De Bello Gallico* ruefully bemoans the charioteers' skill. As the chariots veered close to the enemy lines, the warriors hurled spears at Roman soldiers and gouged them with swords. The warriors then jumped from the chariots to fight on foot while the steady charioteers remained with their chariots poised at a distance, ready to retrieve their masters safely from the fray.[169]

The war chariot is readied for combat, the horses dressed and eager, and the warrior "warped" with the frenzy of the battle. The loyalty of the charioteer steadies the conflict. The charioteer casts a spell over the horses and his comrades-in-arms to disguise them and make ready their presence. From the Ulster Cycle, the story of the champion Cú Chulainn, the Hound of Ulster, and his charioteer, Laeg, epitomizes the loyalty and readiness of the charioteer:

> *"The sickle chariot, friend Laeg," Cúchulainn said, "can you yoke it?" . . . The charioteer rose up then and donned his charioteer's war-harness . . . of stitched deer's leather, light as a breath, kneaded supple and smooth not to hinder his free arm movements . . . his feathery outer mantle [and] his plated, four-pointed, crested battle cap. . . . To set him apart from his master, he placed the charioteer's sign on his brow with his hand: a circle of deep yellow like a single red-gold strip of burning gold shaped on an anvil's edge. He took the long horse-spancel and the ornamented goad in his right hand. In his left hand he grasped the steed-ruling reins that give the charioteer*

control. Then he threw the decorated iron armour-plate over the horses, covering them from head to foot with spears and spit-points, blades, and barbs. Every inch of the chariot bristled. Every angle and corner, front and rear, was a tearing-place.[170]

IF YOU ARE DRAWN TO THIS ORACLE, you are attracting loyal companionship and good counsel. Perhaps you are in a leadership role and you need discerning yet supportive feedback. Perhaps your endeavors are risky and you need cautious and discriminating advice. Perhaps your life is so out of control or in transition that you temporarily need to have a trustworthy person make decisions on your behalf. Perhaps it is sufficient just knowing that others are available to assist you, even if you rarely call on them. Just talking things through with someone sincerely interested in your welfare can be greatly stabilizing and heartening.

The charioteer's great strength is his or her trustworthiness and readiness to help. The more stressed your situation, the more important is reliable counsel and the loyalty of comrades and friends. Choose your confidants wisely, based on their personal qualities, and then seek their counsel, support, and assistance.

~ 62 ~

Treasures

STONE, SPEAR, SWORD, AND CAULDRON

Invoking the Challenges of Mastery and Power

Accomplished in the arts of druidry, the godlike Tuatha Dé Danann came from the isles to the north of the world to invade ancient Ireland. The Tuatha Dé brought four treasures with them: the Stone of Fál, which shrieks when a rightful king sits upon it, the Spear of Lugh, which grants victory, the Sword of Nuada, from which no one escapes, and the Cauldron of the Daghdha, from which none leave hungry. Each treasure represents power and its challenges.

Failius, Goirias, Findias, and Muirias were the four cities of the mythic isles in the northern seas. From the cities' great sages, the Tuatha Dé Danann acquired knowledge of druidry, magic, and prophesy. They invaded ancient Ireland with a great fleet of ships, and upon reaching the western shore, they set their boats on fire and, in so doing, destroyed any hope of returning to the north of the world. Defeating and routing the Fir Bolgs who then lived on the island, the Tuatha Dé controlled all of Ireland and established themselves at the royal court of the high kings of Ireland at Tara. As recorded in the *Book of the Invasions*, which chronicles the successive invasions of Ireland, the Tuatha Dé brought four great treasures to Ireland from the northern isles:

> *From Failias was brought the Lia Fáil which . . . utter[ed] a cry under every king that should take Ireland. From Goirias was brought the spear which Lug [Lugh] had: battle would never go against him who had it in hand. From Findias was brought the sword of Nuadu: no man would escape from it; when it was drawn from its battle-scabbard, there was no resisting it. From Muirias was brought the cauldron of the Dagda [Daghdha]; no company would go from it unsatisfied.*[171]

All four treasures recur in the historical legends of Ireland, and feature prominently in Arthurian legend. By tradition, the Lia Fál (the Stone of Fál) still resides on the hills of Tara in County Meath, the mythic center of Ireland and inaugural site of ancient Irish kings. In a curious blend of ancient and Christian traditions, the *Book of Invasions* tells that the stone made no cry after the birth of Christ.[172]

IF YOU ARE DRAWN TO THIS ORACLE, you are either naturally drawn to power and authority, or your present circumstances require the right use of power. Power is invariably a double-edged sword capable of cutting in two directions. Your skills may involve a natural talent or expertise cultivated over time. Having mastery makes possible important personal accomplishments, expression, and satisfaction. At the same time, by holding authority you also attract circumstances and events that challenge and further develop your skill and authority. Unless you acquire personal qualities equal to your talents and skills, your life situations will become untenable and you will not be able to express the talents and skills you rightfully hold. Consider the possibility that the challenges you attract are actually invitations to bring qualities such as greater awareness, confidence, integrity, savvy, kindness, and equanimity into your nature. Take time to reflect on the particular type of challenges you are presently encountering and the unique qualities needed to meet them successfully.

~ 63 ~

Sun Wheels

TALISMANS

Invoking the Quality of Protection

Sun wheels are signs of protection and healing. Worn as talismans, they protect warriors in battle. Buried with the dead and carved on tombstones, they comfort the dead and illuminate the mysterious journey to the Otherworld. Offered at healing springs and lakes, votive sun wheels are carried to the depths of the earth. Symbolizing the warmth and light of the sun within the fecund earth, they represent healing and protection amid chaos, sorrow, confusion, and pain.

To the ancient Celts, the sun in the sky was a life force rendering fertility to the moist earth, healing to the diseased and sorrowful, and solace in darkness and danger. Iron Age warriors embellished their body armor with sun wheels, seeking the sun's beneficence in danger and giving them courage in battle.[173] Along with personal items suggesting a life after death, small sun wheels were buried with the dead to illuminate the passage in the afterlife, perhaps the journey to the Otherworld. Tombstones in Roman-occupied Alsace in France were decorated with solar symbols, as though to guide and enliven the dead in the Otherworld.[174]

Sun wheels also adorned the bodies of small clay goddess figurines deposited as votives at healing shrines, springs, and lakes and buried with the dead. These figurines were mass-produced, inexpensively available, and crudely fashioned, and may have been popular among women seeking safety in the passage of childbirth. Sometimes referred to as "Venus" figurines, the goddesses were slim-figured and nubile, suggestive of sexuality and fecundity. Offered as prayers and left at curative springs and sacred lakes, these fertile and sun-filled figurines were conveyed to the depths of the Otherworld.[175] This sacred union of the sun and earth brought healing and safety to their Celtic supplicants. At Bath in the southwest of England, the thermal springs of the goddess Aquae Sulis (in Gaelic *sulis* is suggestive of sun) gave comfort to thousands of supplicants before and after the Roman period. The hot springs and the steamy interiors of the shrine inspire a sacred link with sun and earth, a natural vortex of healing and protection to devotees.

Decorating armor and tombstones, worn as amulets, buried with the dead, and accompanying prayers, sun wheels gave hope to the weary and infirm and solace to those in danger.

If you are drawn to this oracle, the brilliance of the sun banishes darkness and chaos and brings you comfort and security.

There are numerous ways to convey the qualities of the sun in your daily life. You might use a sun symbol as a talisman to carry in your pocket, in your purse or bag, or on a chain. Wear an amulet as jewelry, on a necklace, string, or key chain. Keep a symbol of a sun in your office or work area to serve as a reminder, or meditate with the sun as it rises. You might wish to use a candle flame as a focus of meditation. In your imagination, bring light to any darkness and confusion in your life. Allow the outer light to fill the interior reserves of your being. Conduct your daily activities mindful of the light and warmth of the sun.

Sunlight dispels darkness and confusion. The sun as talisman draws the light and warmth of the sun into the chaos, pain, and sorrows of life. Its brilliance will bring you renewed trust and hope.

~ 64 ~

Tir na nÓg

BLESSED ISLE TO THE WEST

Invoking the Qualities of Harmony, Peace, and Blessing

The blessed isles lie off the west coasts of Ireland and Scotland, as if to follow the sun in its homeward path. At the coming of the Celts to Ireland, the ancient Tuatha Dé Danann take shelter there. In *The Voyage of Bran,* Bran and his men wander the seas in search of the Island of Women, a land reveling in harmony, beautiful women, and merriment. In the Fionn Cycle, the young champion Oisín and the princess Niamh of the Golden Hair ride on the sea as if it were a plain to Tir na nÓg, the Land of the Forever Young.

The sanctity of islands to the west harkens back to a mythic time. Dozens of lake islands and islands off the coasts of Scotland and Ireland are revered as sites of homage and pilgrimage, associated with monasteries and abbeys in our time. The prospect of enchanted islands, beckoning the youthful and the adventurous, appearing and disappearing from sight, riding on shining pedestals to glisten in the sun, singing with music to sweeten the air, and bestowing gifts on the virtuous and forsaken has long inspired the Celtic imagination. "West of the sun," for example, is the island of Iona, St. Columba's (Colm Cille) holy strand.[176]

The isles go by many names: Tír fo Thoinn, the Land Under the Waves; Tír Nam Beo, the Land of the Living; Tiirn Ail, the Otherworld; Magh Mór, the Great Plain; Magh Meall, the Pleasant Plain; Tir Tairngire, the Plain of Happiness. Tir na nÓg, the Land of the Forever Young, is a delightful place fit for myths and legends.

Bran mac Feabhail is feasting with his chiefs when a beautiful woman appears from nowhere. She is so lovely that "the company held its breath."[177] Turning toward Bran, she begins to sing:

I bring [an apple] branch of [the Isle of the Happy],
In shape like those you know:
Twigs of white silver are upon it,
Buds of crystal with blossoms.

There is a distant isle,
Around which sea-horses glisten:
A fair course against the white-swelling surge—
Four pedestals uphold it. . . .

Unknown is wailing or treachery
In the homely well-tilled land:
There is nothing rough or harsh,
But sweet music striking the ear.

Without grief, without gloom, without death,
Without any sickness or debility—
That is the sign of [the Isle of the Happy]:
Uncommon is the like of such a marvel.[178]

She admonishes Bran to stop feasting and drinking wine, and asks him to journey across the crystal sea westward to the blessed isle.

Similarly, in the Fionn Cycle from Ireland, Finn and his men, the Fianna, are resting in Lough Lene in Kerry after the bitter battle of Gowra. In the mist of the May morning, Finn and his men send out their dogs to hunt, when suddenly a lovely young woman gallops toward them on a willowy white horse. She is so beautiful that they hold their breath as one. She is Niamh of the Golden Hair and her father is king of Tir na nÓg, the Land of the Forever Young. She tells Finn that she has come because she loves one of his sons, Oisín. So fair is he that rumors have reached all the way to Tir na nÓg. Beckoning Oisín to follow her, she recounts the island's delights:

> *You will never fall ill or grow old there. In my country you will never die. Trees grow tall there and trees bend low with fruit. The land flows with honey and wine, as much as you could ever want. . . . As well as all of this you will get beauty, strength and power. And me for your wife.*[179]

Oisín bids his father, Finn, and all his friends farewell. The horse neighs three times and carries them across the sea, the waves parting before them.

If you are drawn to this oracle, you are becoming more aware of the simple and delightful pleasures of living. The blessings of a land "flowing with milk and honey" in your own terms are coming into your life. Long-held tensions, grudges, hurts, and fears are losing their hold on you. Personal and professional conflicts are being resolved.

Harmony and contentment are replacing disappointment and loss. Your life's work is beginning to manifest in clear and concrete ways.

True paradise is a state of grace. No one can give you joy or take it away. No circumstance can deprive you of your dignity or value. No dream come true is necessarily better than the delight and opportunity to dream. No accord, contract, job, relationship, possession, privilege, or status is better than your inmost vision of yourself, the paradise of being fully content and satisfied. In the Celtic imagination, such a blessing is westward, in the direction of the sun's journey homeward, inward to itself, deep within the pleasures of being fabulously alive.

APPENDIX A

SUMMARY OF ORACLES

Part One: Oracles of the Dark Goddess

The Goddess and Her Attributes

1 ~ Triple-Mother Goddess (Magnificence) *p. 20*
The Triple-Mother Goddess, commonly manifesting as maiden, mother, and crone, signifies the magnificence of Mother Earth in giving life. Expressing herself in all aspects of life, she encompasses all ages, polarities, and expressions. Her qualities are majesty, generativity, and an inner connection with the life-giving sovereignty of the earth.

2 ~ Cauldron of Creation (Source) *p. 23*
The womb (or cauldron) of the goddess is the source of creation. As the inexhaustible cauldron, she restores the dead to life. Her presence signals a need for repose, rest, and a complete overhaul of life energies before life is regenerated again.

3 ~ Mother Goddess Carrying Children/Food (Well-Being) *p. 26*
The goddess of care-giving provides comfort, ease, and contentment in the home and wherever she goes. Her qualities provide for daily nurturance and the necessities of life and support for our physical and emotional fulfillment.

4 ~ The Sacred Three (Seeing in All Directions) *p. 29*
Odd numbers, multiples of three, and the triple spirals are sacred symbols in the Celtic world. Triplication of divine figures signifies the all-seeing and unifying presence of the spirit world. Look for the wider circumstances behind events.

The Dark Goddess of Change

5 ~ Hag, the Initiator (Beginnings) *p. 33*
The hag initiates change and transformation, and signals the potential for significant change and transformation in relationships and the affairs of everyday life. Her often terrifying appearance is a test of your readiness for change.

6 ~ The Morrigán, the Raven Goddess (Chaos) *p. 36*
The Morrigán signals the presence of sex, lovemaking, chaos, and often death to a particular way of being. Chaos clears the way for transformation. Often appearing in disguise, her qualities are confusion, chaos, destruction or death, and rapid change.

7 ~ Brigit, the Snake and Fire Goddess (Transformation) *p. 39*
The snake goddess is associated with midwifery, smithing, and the fostering of the creative arts. Her capacity for change and renewal inspires creativity in challenging situations, and enhances our capacity to meet old circumstances with renewed vision. Her qualities are imagination, intuition, and vision.

8 ~ Epona, the Horse Goddess (Safe Passage) *p. 42*
The horse goddess Epona carries the dead across the chasm of death into another realm of life. She carries and accompanies us across the chasms of transition and change. Her qualities bring guidance, protection, and safety in transitions.

The Dark Goddess and Her Animals

9 ~ Bear (Fierce Femininity) *p. 45*
The wild bear of the forest is the expression of motherly devotion and loyalty to family and kin. In times of provocation and danger, the mother bear protects and defends her young without regard to her own safety. Her actions are swift and unselfish.

10 ~ Cow (Inexhaustible Supply) *p. 48*
The cow signifies the joy and contentment found in open-hearted giving and receiving of nurturance. The qualities of the cow are nurturance, generosity, compassion, and hospitality to friends and strangers alike.

11 ~ Lap Dog, Hound of the Goddess (Intimacy with Self) *p. 51*
The lap dog brings healing and renewal to the inmost self. Old habits and traumas may resolve effortlessly. The lap dog's presence signifies an auspicious time to bring loving attention to our deep emotional and spiritual natures.

12 ~ Mare (Healing the Wounds of Abandonment, Betrayal, and Loss of Trust) *p. 54*
The mare signifies the healing of emotional and psychological wounding, especially in close relationships. By nourishing and comforting our sense of loss, trust in the future is restored. Her qualities are confidence and hope.

Appendix A

Sacred Union

13 ~ Coupling of Earth and Sky (Unlimited Possibilities) p. 57
The sexual coupling of goddesses with gods and mortal men represents the union of sacred polarities—feminine and masculine, earth and sky, darkness with light—and the procreation of unlimited possibilities. Success requires steady development.

14 ~ Sacred King (The Oath) p. 60
The sacred king represents the successful union of the sovereign goddess with a mortal king. If the king is faithful to his oath, the people prosper. The sacred king signifies honorable and responsible actions.

15 ~ Divine Couple (Union) p. 63
The divine couple promotes the health and well-being of the family, household, or locale and assures the continuity of life, even after death. The presence of the divine couple brings domestic harmony, prosperity, and success in business and commerce.

16 ~ Wondrous Child (Promise) p. 66
The wondrous child represents promise, hope in the future, and the rekindling of spiritual life. The new life is innocent, potential, and incomplete. The qualities of newborn innocence and inner development require safety and long stretches of unencumbered time.

Part Two: Oracles of Nature's Wisdoms

Animals

17 ~ Boar (Fearless in Conflict) p. 70
The wild boar or pig is a fierce and indomitable creature symbolizing war and conflict. The fury of an enraged boar or army is rightly feared. The qualities of the boar are fierceness, power, and unassailable strength.

18 ~ Water Horses (Magical Encounters) p. 74
Water horses, or sea horses, are magical horses riding over the seas or appearing from the depths of inland lochs. Water horses appear magically and swiftly. Their presence signifies masculine strength and beauty.

19 ~ Raven (Truth-telling and Prophesy) p. 77
Ravens and crows represent the power of speaking the truth—and sometimes the power of prophesy. The raven brings truthfulness, clarity, and insight into the nature of a relationship, event, or situation. Tell the truth in the present situation.

20 ~ Salmon (Knowledge) *p. 80*
As a magical creature of the waters that is close to powers of the Otherworld, the salmon brings knowledge and wisdom, expressing them through the creative arts, especially poetry, prose, and singing. Ancient bards were inspired by tasting the salmon of knowledge.

Sovereignty in the Animal Realm

21 ~ Cernunnos, Antlered God (Lord of the Animals) *p. 83*
God and guardian of the animal realm, Cernunnos's authority is heralded by wearing the antlers of the deer. He provides sustenance and protection for the animals under his care. His qualities are generosity and magnanimity.

22 ~ Utterly Stag (Wild Nature) *p. 86*
The king of the forest, the stag deer represents dignity and potency in life. By bringing the quality of dignity to passion, the stag focuses the passionate, wild, and sometimes unruly forces within and outside our own natures.

23 ~ Ram-horned Snake (Shape-shifting) *p. 89*
The ram-horned serpent signifies the capacity to change form, consciousness, or action spontaneously and quickly. Close to the earth and in touch with what is needed, the ram-horned serpent freely changes action, mood, form, and consciousness.

24 ~ Banishing of Snakes (Loss of Hope/Regenerative Power) *p. 92*
The break in connection with the powers governed by the Otherworld is symbolized in the banishing of snakes (attributed to St. Patrick) in Ireland. This oracle signifies a loss of a vital connection with the powers of the physical and natural world and invites reconnection.

Ancient Trees and Scepters

25 ~ Oak (The Ancient Wood) *p. 95*
Oaks are among the long-lived trees, signifying the presence of the ages and the long memory of trees. They symbolize life and rebirth and the connection between earth and sky. Ancient groves inspire celebration of the continuity of life.

26 ~ Rowan, Mountain Ash (The Alchemical Wand) *p. 98*
The rowan and its red berries in winter are connected with the Otherworld. Twigs are sometimes worn on clothing for protection from malevolent spirits.

Rowan berries signal chthonic protection, divination, good luck, and sometimes healing and the giving of wisdom.

27 ~ Hazel (The Divining Rod) *p. 101*
The hazel is the wood used for divination in everyday life and specifically in divining for water beneath the ground. Because of its purity, the hazel lends guidance and direction to the affairs of life. Its presence signals a time of reflection and concentration.

28 ~ Thorn Tree (The Sacred Sign) *p. 104*
The thorn tree is sacred and inviolable. Cutting one down brings misfortune for dishonoring the habitats of the faeries of the underground. Take care not to disturb something sacred. Attend to purifying actions and intentions, including actions in the past.

Elemental Spirits

29 ~ Leprechauns (Earth) *p. 107*
Leprechauns represent the playful and resourceful qualities of the earth. By poking fun at our desire for riches, the leprechauns teach us detachment and equanimity in relationship to material wealth and status.

30 ~ Faery Wind (Air) *p. 111*
The faery winds and whirlwinds of late summer burst forth suddenly and take a part of the harvest to the Otherworld. The winds signify the need to offer a part of our resources to the spirit world. The winds urge us to avoid indulgence and to serve our communities generously.

31 ~ Willy the Wisp—Jack O' Lantern (Fire) *p. 114*
Willy the Wisp is too bad for heaven and too clever for hell. He therefore forever wanders the countryside with a wisp of light. Using the creativity of fire unwisely or selfishly brings misfortune. Seek to use creativity and talent with generosity and compassion.

32 ~ Mermaids and Selkies (Water) *p. 117*
Mermaids and selkies are female enchantresses of the seas. Often marrying human men, they eventually return to the sea. They signify the qualities of femininity, longing, beauty, and wonder in life.

Part Three: Oracles from the Otherworld

The Earth and the Fiery Otherworld

33 ~ Sovereignty (Voluptuous Authority) *p. 122*
Sovereignty is personified by the mother goddess who grants sovereignty to rightful kings. The earth's power originates in her hot and fiery interior, giving the earth's surface its lively, sensuous, and voluptuous qualities. Her presence signifies enthusiasm and activity.

34 ~ Power of Place (Calling in the Spirit of Place) *p. 125*
The landscape—its hills, glens, plains, shorelines, nooks, and crannies—are the features of the body of the mother goddess, the earth. Place-names honor the unique qualities and lore of place. Similarly, honoring the power of place situates us in the passage of time.

35 ~ Spirit of Mountains (Breasts of the Goddess) *p. 128*
Certain mountains, such as the Paps of Anu in Ireland, signify the breasts of the mother goddess, the earth. Overflowing in generosity, they symbolize the qualities of mercy, forgiveness, and impartiality in human life.

36 ~ Cauldron of the Otherworld (Alchemy) *p. 131*
The brewing cauldron symbolizes the goddess's powers of replenishment in everyday life. In the brewing of earth's elements, alchemy and medicine are formed. The cauldron conveys healing to the body and emotions, and wisdom to actions. Lost aspects of the self may be returned.

Gateways to the Otherworld

37 ~ Nymphs (Healing) *p. 134*
The nymphlike goddesses of healing springs are sometimes nurturing and soothing, or playfully erotic. They bring healing and loving attention to our physical bodies. Their qualities include the giving and receiving of intimacy.

38 ~ Wells and Thermal Springs (Returning to the Source) *p. 137*
Wells and thermal springs are orifices or gateways to the sacred, hot interior of the goddess earth. Her presence marks strength and capacity in our personal and spiritual lives and the desire to express inner changes in our everyday lives.

39 ~ The Under Tree (Taking Root in the Otherworld) *p. 140*
The Under Tree extends its trunk and opens its branches toward the sky and into the Otherworld. It represents our capacity to expand and stand strong in the hidden and unknown aspects of our nature and to nourish their graceful expression.

40 ~ Chambers in the Earth (Rhythms of the Otherworld) *p. 143*
Caves and subterranean chambers, natural or dug out of the ground, represent our desire to maintain an intimate connection to the Otherworld. Although our actions may seem slow or sluggish to others, steady progress is occurring in the rhythm common to the Otherworld.

Beings Between the Worlds

41 ~ Green Man (Renewal of the Earth) *p. 146*
The face and features of the Green Man are formed of leaves. He represents the masculine role in sexual coupling and fertility and the flowering of life and talent. Progress is uncluttered and easy. His qualities are innocence, success, and easy progress.

42 ~ Changeling (Exchange Between Worlds) *p. 149*
The Changeling represents the exchange between worlds. Some people are faeries or have otherworldly characteristics. Some of them bring exceptional talents and skills. Received and used wisely, an exchange between the worlds brings otherworldly knowing.

43 ~ Pooka (The Trickster) *p. 152*
From the Pooka, a goblin and trickster of the Otherworld, expect the unusual. The Pooka is known to take humans for a ride and dump them. He is not what he appears to be. Be open to unforeseen experiences, circumstances, or insight.

44 ~ Banshee (The Call Between Worlds) *p. 155*
The banshee's call is a manifestation of the threshold of significant life change, including the transition through death and death to old ways of living. She brings continuity between the worlds. Her qualities are certainty, reassurance, and hope.

The Faery World

45 ~ *Faery Hill (The Hidden World of Faeries)* *p. 158*
By legend, the faeries are the descendants of the Tuatha Dé Danann, a godlike race who once inhabited Ireland. They now reside beneath the ground inside hills and mounds in the countryside. Their presence signifies inspiration.

46 ~ *Faeries of Mischief and Play* *p. 161*
Faeries are mischievous, playful, and like to poke fun at human seriousness. They favor mischief and merrymaking. Their presence brings playfulness, frolic, mischief, humor, laughter, and fun into life.

47 ~ *Faeries of Music, Dance, and the Performing Arts* *p. 164*
Faeries love to dance, sing, and play music, and sometimes gift musicians (especially fiddlers and pipers) with great talent in fiddling or piping. Their presence brings talents and resources in the pleasures of dancing, singing, and music.

48 ~ *Faery Lover (Sensuality)* *p. 168*
The faery lover (suitor) is a beautiful man or woman who comes (often in the night) to rouse and seduce us. The faery lover's presence signifies unexpected pleasure and delight, and sometimes danger.

Part Four: Oracles of Darkness and Light

Nighttime Stories and Relations

49 ~ *Nightfall (Thresholds and Beginnings)* *p. 172*
Dusk is the beginning of each new day. In the stillness of night, we cross the threshold of beginning anew. We discover ourselves in the dark, as if carved from the night. Inspiration begins at dusk and expands while protected by the night.

50 ~ *Hearth and Family (Right Relations)* *p. 175*
In the cold lands in the north of Europe and elsewhere, family and friends gather near the fire at night. The warmth of the fire and the closeness of family, friends, and community is strengthened and valued.

51 ~ *Bards (Storytelling)* *p. 178*
Around a fire, the old stories are told again. In the telling of stories the past more consciously bears upon the present. Set against the long story of life, the familiar and unusual mingle to form the contours and patterns of our lives.

52 ~ Presence of Ancestors (The Ancient Ones) *p. 181*
Often our ancestors wish to support and accompany our actions and our story-telling, to give guidance and add to our store of wisdom. Their presence adds to our strength and vigor. Particular ancestors may be especially present.

Luminous Spirits of the Night and Death

53 ~ New Moon (Wisdoms of the Heart) *p. 184*
The new moon represents the wisdoms of the heart, which come with emotional and spiritual maturity. Spiritual traditions everywhere tell of the compassionate wisdoms (or intelligence) of the heart. Knowledge is acquired from the implicit and tacit meanings of things in their essence.

54 ~ Esus Cutting the Tree (Sacrifice) *p. 187*
A living tree signifies the source of life and is therefore sacred. The ritual of cutting or sacrificing a tree represents relinquishing the practiced and familiar for the new and unknown. Cutting the tree signifies surrender of the old and receptivity to the new.

55 ~ Hammer God (Scepter of Authority and Choice) *p. 190*
The Hammer God is primarily a tribal father god, wielding his hammer or mallet as a symbol of authority and command. He is mature and kindly, yet his presence signifies the need to consider options wisely and make sound, discriminating decisions.

56 ~ Head (Immortality) *p. 193*
For the Celts, and many other indigenous peoples, the head carries the essence of a person—even after death. Considering what we will leave to future generations after our death often gives maturity and perspective to daily activities.

Beings of Light

57 ~ Sun God (God of the Sky) *p. 196*
The power and return of the sun has been acclaimed and honored for thousands of years. The warmth and light of the sun kindles the life-giving potential of the earth's biosphere. The sun's qualities are majesty, radiance, fertility, and beauty.

58 ~ Taranis (God of Lightning and Thunder) *p. 199*
Taranis, the god of lightning and thunder, announces the swift and action-packed authority of the sky world. His actions can be benevolent or destructive. His presence signifies a need to be vigilant and to be ready to act swiftly.

59 ~ Oengus/Mabon (Youthful Champion, Son of Light) *p. 201*
Oengus is one of the Tuatha Dé Danann, son of a secret union between Daghdha and Bóinn, the river goddess. Falling in love with a girl he sees in a dream, Oengus finds her and heroically wins her. Oengus and his counterpart in the Welsh tradition, Mabon, represent the youthful championing of innocence, virtue, and love.

60 ~ Lugh/Lludd (Warrior, the Shining One) *p. 204*
Lugh, the master of all arts, is one of the Tuatha Dé Danaan and a great warrior of the Irish mythological cycle. As foretold by a druid, he kills his own grandfather, Balor of the Evil Eye. A warrior's quality is mastery.

Symbols of Light and Rescue

61 ~ Charioteer / The Chariot (Rescue from Danger) *p. 207*
The charioteer is a loyal companion who comes quickly to rescue us from danger. While the warrior fights, the charioteer keeps the chariot slightly apart from the fray, helping the warrior make a hasty retreat. The charioteer's qualities are trustworthiness and loyalty.

62 ~ Treasures (Stone, Spear, Sword, and Cauldron) *p. 210*
The four treasures brought by the Tuatha Dé Danann to Ireland are the Stone of Fál, the Spear of Lugh, the Sword of Nuada, and the Cauldron of the Daghdha. Each treasure in turn signals power and a challenge for further development of your character.

63 ~ Sun Wheels (Talismans) *p. 213*
Like the sun itself, sunlight gives protection and warmth. Carved or crudely fashioned sun wheels are talismans drawing the light and warmth of the sun into the chaos, pain, and sorrow of life—and even into death. The sun wheel's qualities are trust and hope.

64 ~ Tir na nÓg (Blessed Isle to the West) *p. 216*
The Tir na nÓg is one of many blessed and magical isles to the west. It is the land of the forever young, reveling in beauty, merriment, and harmony. Its qualities are joy, pleasure, peace, and blessing.

APPENDIX B

NUMBER SEQUENCES FOR CELTIC ORACLES

Oracle	First Cast	Second Cast	Third Cast
1	1	1	1
2	1	1	2
3	1	1	3
4	1	1	4
5	1	2	1
6	1	2	2
7	1	2	3
8	1	2	4
9	1	3	1
10	1	3	2
11	1	3	3
12	1	3	4
13	1	4	1
14	1	4	2
15	1	4	3
16	1	4	4
17	2	1	1
18	2	1	2
19	2	1	3
20	2	1	4
21	2	2	1
22	2	2	2
23	2	2	3
24	2	2	4
25	2	3	1
26	2	3	2
27	2	3	3
28	2	3	4

Number Sequences

29	2	4	1
30	2	4	2
31	2	4	3
32	2	4	4
33	3	1	1
34	3	1	2
35	3	1	3
36	3	1	4
37	3	2	1
38	3	2	2
39	3	2	3
40	3	2	4
41	3	3	1
42	3	3	2
43	3	3	3
44	3	3	4
45	3	4	1
46	3	4	2
47	3	4	3
48	3	4	4
49	4	1	1
50	4	1	2
51	4	1	3
52	4	1	4
53	4	2	1
54	4	2	2
55	4	2	3
56	4	2	4
57	4	3	1
58	4	3	2
59	4	3	3
60	4	3	4
61	4	4	1
62	4	4	2
63	4	4	3
64	4	4	4

SELECTED CELTIC BIBLIOGRAPHY

Anderson, William. *Green Man: The Archetype of Our Oneness with the Earth*. London/San Francisco: HarperCollins, 1990.

Bamford, Christopher, and William Parker March. *Celtic Christianity: Ecology and Holiness*. Hudson, N.Y.: Lindisfarne Press, 1982.

Byrne, Francis John. *Irish Kings and High-Kings*. London: Batsford, 1973.

Carmichael, Alexander. *Carmina Gadelica: Hymns and Incantations with Illustrative Notes on Words, Rites, and Customs, Dying and Obsolete: Orally Collected in the Highlands and Islands of Scotland and Translated into English*, vol. 1–6. Vol. 1–2, ed. Elizabeth Catherine Carmichael (1900/1984); vol. 3 (1940) and vol. 4 (1988), ed. James Carmichael Watson; vol. 5, ed. Angus Matheson (1987); vol. 6, ed. Angus Matheson (1988). Edinburgh: Scottish Academic Press.

Chadwick, Nora. *The Celts*. New York/London: Penguin Books, 1971.

Condgren, Mary. *The Serpent and The Goddess: Women, Religion, and Power in Celtic Ireland*. San Francisco: HarperCollins, 1989.

Cross, Tom Peete, and Clark Harvis Slover. *Ancient Irish Tales*. New York: Henry Holt, 1936.

Dames, Michael. *Mythic Ireland*. New York/London: Thames and Hudson, 1992.

Davies, Sioned. *The Four Branches of the Mabinogi*. Llandysul: Gomer Press, 1993.

De Waal, Esther, ed. *The Celtic Vision*. Petersham, MA/London: St. Bede's Publications/Daron, Longman & Todd, 1988.

Eisner, Sigmund. *A Tale of Wonder*. Wexford, England: John English, 1957.

Flower, Robin. *The Western Island or the Great Basket*. Oxford: The Clarendon Press, 1944.

———. *The Irish Tradition*. Oxford: Oxford University Press, 1947.

Ford, Patrick K., trans. and ed. *The Mabinogi and Other Medieval Welsh Tales*. Berkeley/Los Angeles/London: University of California Press, 1977.

Gantz, Jeffrey, trans. *The Mabinogion*. New York: Dorset Press, 1976.

Glob, Peter Vilhelm. *The Bog People*. London: Faber and Faber, 1969.

Graves, Robert. *The White Goddess: A Historical Grammar of Poetic Myth*. New York: Moonday Press; Farrar, Straus & Giroux, 1948/1966.

Gray, Elizabeth A. *Cath Maig Tuired: The Second Battle of Mag Tuired*. Dublin: Irish Texts Society, 1982.

Green, David H. *An Anthology of Irish Literature*. New York: The Modern Library, 1954.

Green, Miranda. *Symbol and Image in Celtic Religious Art*. London/New York: Routledge, 1989.

———. *A Dictionary of Celtic Myth and Legend*. London: Thames & Hudson, 1992.

———. *Animals in Celtic Life and Myth*. London/New York: Routledge, 1992.

———. *Celtic Myths*. London/Austin, Texas: British Museum Press/University of Texas Press, 1993.

———. *Celtic Goddesses: Warriors, Virgins and Mothers*. New York: George Braziller, 1995.

Guest, Lady Charlotte, ed. and trans. *The Mabinogion*. London: Bernard Quaritch, 1877. Facsimile ed., Cardiff, Wales: John Jones Cardiff, Ltd., 1977 (paperback ed., Mineola, N.Y.: Dover Publications, 1997).

Harbison, Peter. *Pilgrimage in Ireland: The Monuments and the People*. Syracuse, N.Y.: Syracuse University Press, 1991.

Heaney, Marie. *Over Nine Waves: A Book of Irish Legends*. London/Boston: Faber and Faber, 1994.

Heaney, Seamus. *Preoccupations: Selected Prose*. London/Boston: Faber and Faber, 1980.

Henken, Elissa R. *Traditions of the Welsh Saints*. Cambridge: Boydell & Brewer, 1987.

Hyde, Douglas. *A Literary History of Ireland from Earliest Times to the Present Day*. London: T. F. Unwin, 1899/1901.

Jones, Francis. *The Holy Wells of Wales*. Cardiff, Wales: University of Wales Press, 1954.

Keightley, Thomas. *The Fairy Mythology*. London: H. G. Bohm, 1860.

Kinsella, Thomas, ed. *The New Oxford Book of Irish Verse*. Oxford: Oxford University Press, 1986.

Kinsella, Thomas, trans. *The Táin*, from the Irish epic *Táin Bó Cuailnge*. Oxford: Oxford University Press, 1969.

Lebor Gabála Érenn. *The Book of the Taking of Ireland, Part IV*. Ed. and trans. Robert Alexander Stewart MacAlister. Dublin: Published for Irish Texts Society by the Educational Co. of Ireland, 1941.

———. *The Book of the Taking of Ireland, Part V*. Ed. and trans. Robert Alexander Stewart MacAlister. Dublin: Published for Irish Texts Society by the Educational Co. of Ireland, 1956.

Mackey, James P. *An Introduction to Celtic Christianity*. Edinburgh: T. & T. Clark, 1989.

Markale, Jean. *The Celts: Uncovering the Mythic and Historic Origins of Western Culture*. Rochester, VT: Inner Traditions International, 1993.

Matthews, Caitlín. *Mabon and the Mysteries of Britain: An Exploration of the Mabinogion*. London/New York: Arkana, 1987.

———. *Arthur and the Sovereignty of Britain: King and Goddess in the Mabinogion*. London: Arkana, 1989.

———. *The Celtic Tradition*. Rocksport, Mass.: Element, 1989.

Matthews, John. *Taliesin: Shamanism and the Bardic Mysteries in Britain and Ireland*. London: The Aquarian Press/HarperCollins, 1991.

Meyer, Kuno, trans. *Ancient Irish Poetry*. London: Constable, 1913/1994.

Meyer, Kuno, and Alfred Nutt. *The Voyage of Bran, Son of Febal*. London: AMS Press, 1895.

Montague, John, ed. *The Faber Book of Irish Verse*. London: Faber and Faber, 1974.

Mullin, Kay N. *A Wondrous Land: The Faery Faith in Ireland*. Freshfield, Chieveley, Berks, U.K.: Capall Bann Publishers, 1997.

Murray, Patrick, ed. *The Deer's Cry: A Treasury of Irish Religious Verse*. Co. Dublin: Four Courts Press, 1986.

Ní Dhomhnaill, Nuala. *Selected Poems*, trans. Michael Hartnett. Dublin: New Island Books/Raven Arts Press, 1988/1993.

Ó Catháin, Séamus, ed. and trans. *The Festival of Brigit: Celtic Goddess and Holy Woman*. Blackrock, Co. Dublin: DBA Publications, 1995.

———. *An Hour by the Hearth: Stories Told by Pádraig Eoghain Phádraig Mac an Luain*. Dublin: University College Dublin, 1985.

O'Curry, Eugene. "The Three Most Sorrowful Tales of Erinn." *Atlantis* 4 (1958).

Ó Duilearga, Séamus. *Seán Ó Conáill's Book: Stories and Traditions from Iveragh*, trans. Máire MacNeill. Dublin: University College, 1981.

Ó hEachaidh, Seán. *Fairy Legends from Donegal*, trans. Máire MacNeill. Dublin: Comhairle Béaloideas Éireann, University College, 1977.

O'Rahilly, Thomas F. *Early Irish History and Mythology*. Dublin: Dublin Institute for Advanced Studies, 1946.

Ó Searcaigh, Cathal. *Homecoming: Selected Poems*, ed. Gabriel Fitzmaurice. Connemara, Ireland: Cló Iar-Chonnachta, Indreabhán, 1993.

O'Sullivan, Donal, and Míchael Ó Súilleabháin, eds. *Bunting's Ancient Music of Ireland*. Cork, Ireland: Cork University Press, 1983.

Powell, Thomas George Eyre. *The Celts*. London: Thames & Hudson, 1958.

Sellner, Edward C. *Wisdom of the Celtic Saints*. Notre Dame, Ind.: Ave Maria Press, 1993.

Stewart, Robert J. *Celtic Gods and Celtic Goddesses*. London: Blandford, 1990.

Thomas, Jenkyn W. *The Welsh Fairy Book*. Cardiff: University of Wales Press, 1995.

Twohig, Elizabeth Shee. *Irish Megalithic Tombs*. Princess Risborough, Buckinghamshire, U.K.: Shire Archaeology, 1990.

ENDNOTES

1. Marija Gimbutas, *The Goddesses and Gods of Old Europe: Myths and Cult Images* (Berkeley/Los Angeles: University of California Press, 1982).
2. *New Jerusalem Bible*. (Garden City, N.Y.: Doubleday & Company, 1985), 373 notes.
3. Alexander Carmichael, *Carmina Gadelica: Hymns and Incantations with Illustrative Notes on Words, Rites, and Customs, Dying and Obsolete: Orally Collected in the Highlands and Islands of Scotland and Translated into English* (Edinburgh: Scottish Academic Press 1900/1984), vol. 2, 158.
4. Ibid., 5:288–89.
5. Ibid., 2:159.
6. Ibid., 5:292.
7. Ibid., 2:159.
8. Lebor Gabála Érenn, *The Book of the Taking of Ireland, Part V*, ed. and trans. Robert Alexander Stewart MacAlister and Eoin Mac Néill (Dublin: Published for the Irish Texts Society by the Educational Co. of Ireland, 1938), 36–37.
9. Nuala Ní Dhomhnaill, "Mór Hatching," in *Selected Poems*, trans. Michael Hartnett (Dublin: New Island Books/Raven Arts Press, 1988/1993), 33.
10. Miranda Green, *Celtic Myths* (London/Austin, Texas: British Museum Press/University of Texas Press, 1993), 76.
11. Patrick K. Ford, trans. and ed., *The Mabinogion and Other Medieval Welsh Tales* (Berkeley/Los Angeles: University of California Press, 1977), 63.
12. Robert Graves, *The White Goddess: A Historical Grammar of Poetic Myth* (New York: Moonday Press, Farrar, Straus & Giroux, 1948/1966), 13.
13. Miranda Green, *Symbol and Image in Celtic Religious Art* (London/New York: Routledge, 1989), 179, 204.
14. Ibid., 171–79.
15. Carmichael, *Carmina Gadelica*, 1:234–35.
16. Nuala Ní Dhomhnaill, "Donncha Dí's Testimony," in *Selected Poems*, trans. Michael Hartnett (Dublin: New Island Books/Raven Arts Press, 1988/1993), 35.
17. For a summary of tales of the Loathy Lady, see Sigmund Eisner,

A *Tale of Wonder* (Wexford, England: John English and Co., 1957), 17–30.

18. John Matthews, *Taliesin: Shamanism and the Bardic Mysteries in Britain and Ireland* (London: The Aquarian Press/HarperCollins, 1991), 77.
19. Elizabeth A. Gray, ed., *Cath Maig Tuired: The Second Battle of Mag Tuired* (Dublin: Irish Texts Society, 1982), 72.
20. Thomas Kinsella., trans., *The Táin*, from the Irish epic *Táin Bó Cuailnge* (Oxford: Oxford University Press, 1969), 238–39.
21. Marie Heaney, *Over Nine Waves: A Book of Irish Legends* (London/Boston: Faber and Faber, 1994), 148.
22. Carmichael, *Carmina Gadelica*, 3:163.
23. Ibid., 1:169.
24. Miranda Green, *Symbol and Image in Celtic Religious Art* (London/New York: Routledge, 1989), 23–24.
25. Ibid., 18.
26. Jeffrey Gantz, trans., *The Mabinogion* (New York: Dorset Press, 1976), 52–54.
27. Green, *Symbol and Image in Celtic Religious Art*, 134.
28. Marija Gimbutas, *The Goddesses and Gods of Old Europe: Myths and Cult Images* (Berkeley/Los Angeles: University of California Press, 1982), 196.
29. Miranda Green, *Celtic Goddesses: Warriors, Virgins and Mothers* (New York: George Braziller, 1995), 166–67.
30. Séamus Ó Catháin, *The Festival of Brigit: Celtic Goddess and Holy Woman* (Blackrock, Co. Dublin: DBA Publications, 1995), 5.
31. Irish Folklore Department, University College Dublin, *Main Manuscript*, 903:79–80. Collected by Seán Ó Súilleabháin (O'Sullivan) from Mary O'Toole, Carrowmore, Louisburgh, Co. Mayo, in a letter dated May 26, 1942.
32. Jenkyn W. Thomas, *The Welsh Fairy Book* (Cardiff, Wales: University of Wales Press, 1995), 280.
33. Jeffrey Gantz, trans., *The Mabinogion* (New York: Dorset Press, 1976), 46–47.
34. Green, *Symbol and Image in Celtic Religious Art*, 30, 49.
35. Miranda Green, *Animals in Celtic Life and Myth* (London/New York: Routledge, 1992), 200–202.
36. Ibid., 153–56.
37. Gantz, *The Mabinogion*, 60.
38. Francis John Byrne, *Irish Kings and High-Kings* (London: Batsford, 1973), 17.
39. Miranda Green, *Celtic Myths* (London/Austin, Texas: British Museum Press/University of Texas Press, 1993), 19.

40. Green, *Symbol and Image in Celtic Religious Art*, 46–54.
41. Miranda Green, *Celtic Goddesses: Warriors, Virgins and Mothers* (New York: George Braziller, 1995), 125–28.
42. John Matthews, "The Consolation of Elffin," trans. John and Caitlín Matthews, in *Taliesin: Shamanism and the Bardic Mysteries in Britain and Ireland* (London: Aquarian Press/HarperCollins, 1991), 280.
43. Green, *Animals in Celtic Life and Myth*, 91.
44. Ibid., 116.
45. Lady Charlotte Guest, ed. and trans., "Math, Song of Mathonwy," in *The Mabinogion* (London: Bernard Quaritch, 1877/facsimile ed. Cardiff, Wales: John Jones Cardiff, Ltd., 1977), 414–45.
46. Green, *Celtic Myths*, 35–36.
47. Marie Heaney, *Over Nine Waves: A Book of Irish Legends* (London/ Boston: Faber and Faber, 1994), 59.
48. Irish Folklore Department, University College Dublin, *Schools' Manuscript*, 599:234–36. Quin, Co. Clare. Collected by Liam Mac Clúin.
49. Irish Folklore Department, University College Dublin, *Schools' Manuscript*, 163:326–27. Written by Linda Gibson from Rathlee, Co. Sligo. Told by Patrick Devaney from Co. Sligo.
50. Green, *Symbol and Image in Celtic Religious Art*, 26, 42, 48.
51. Green, *Animals in Celtic Life and Myth*, 161.
52. Ibid., 151.
53. Green, *Symbol and Image in Celtic Religious Art*, 27.
54. Heaney, *Over Nine Waves: A Book of Irish Legends*, 152.
55. Ibid., 162–63.
56. Green, *Animals in Celtic Life and Myth*, 146–48.
57. Green, *Symbol and Image in Celtic Religious Art*, 95–96.
58. Lady Charlotte Guest, ed. and trans., "The Lady of the Fountain," in *The Mabinogion* (London: Bernard Quaritch, 1877/facsimile ed. Cardiff, Wales: John Jones Cardiff, Ltd., 1977), 6–7.
59. Green, *Symbol and Image in Celtic Religious Art*, 134–35.
60. Green, *Celtic Goddesses: Warriors, Virgins and Mothers*, 230.
61. Green, *Symbol and Image in Celtic Religious Art*, 88.
62. Green, *Celtic Goddesses: Warriors, Virgins and Mothers*, 167.
63. Christopher Bamford and William Parker Marsh, *Celtic Christianity: Ecology and Holiness* (Hudson, N.Y.: Lindisfarne Press, 1982), 46–47.
64. John Matthews, "Gad Goddeu," trans. John and Caitlín Matthews, in *Taliesin: Shamanism and the Bardic Mysteries in Britain and Ireland* (London: Aquarian

Press/HarperCollins, 1991), 296–97.

65. Green, *Animals in Celtic Life and Myth*, 227.
66. Michael Dames, *Mythic Ireland* (New York/London: Thames & Hudson, 1992), 167–68.
67. Peter Harbison, *Pilgrimage in Ireland: The Monuments and the People* (Syracuse, N.Y.: Syracuse University Press, 1991), 67–70.
68. Green, *Celtic Myths*, 50–51, 65–66, 78.
69. Cathal Ó Searcaigh, "Mountain Woman," trans. Lillis Ó Laoire, in *Homecoming: Selected Poems*, ed. Gabriel Fitzmaurice (Connemara, Ireland: Cló Iar-Chonnachta, Indreabhán, 1993), 116–19.
70. Heaney, *Over Nine Waves: A Book of Irish Legends*, 23.
71. Thomas Keightley, *The Fairy Mythology* (London: H. G. Bohm, 1860), 354–55.
72. Patricia Lysaght, "Trees in Irish Folk Tradition," *Irish Biological Records Centre Newsletter* 14:22–39 (1979).
73. Irish Folklore Department, University College Dublin, *Main Manuscript*, 815:13. Recorded by P. J. Gaynor, Bailieboro, Co. Cavan, from Charles King, Murmud, Lurgan, Virginia, Co. Cavan, storyteller and farmer, age 60.
74. Heaney, *Over Nine Waves: A Book of Irish Legends*, 167–68.
75. Patricia Lysaght, "Trees in Irish Folk Tradition," *Irish Biological Records Centre Newsletter*, 14:38 (1979).
76. Kay N. Mullin, *A Wondrous Land: The Faery Faith in Ireland* (Freshfield, Chieveley, Berks, U.K.: Capall Bann Publishers, 1997), 89–90.
77. Diarmuid Ó Gilláin, "The Leipreachán and Fairies, Dwarfs, and the Household Familiar: A Comparative Study," *Béaloideas* 52 (1984):75–150.
78. Irish Folklore Department, University College Dublin, *Main Manuscript*, 407:233.
79. Irish Folklore Department, University College Dublin, *Main Manuscript*, 90:96.
80. Seán Ó hEachaidh, *Fairy Legends from Donegal*, trans. Máire MacNeill (Dublin: Comhairle Béaloideas Éireann, University College, 1977), 269.
81. Séamus Ó Duilearga, *Seán Ó Conaill's Book: Stories and Traditions from Iveragh*, trans. Máire MacNeill (Dublin: University College, 1981), 271.
82. Irish Folklore Department, University College Dublin, *Main Manuscript*, 169:498–500. From Ballybobaneen, Co. Donegal. Collected in 1935 by Liam MacMeanman from Tom Gallen.
83. Irish Folklore Department, University College Dublin, *Main Manuscript*, 744:27–29. From

Annasasul, Co. Derry. Collected by P. Ó. Súilleabháin.

84. Irish Folklore Department, University College Dublin, *Main Manuscript*, 462:313. From Tinryland, Co. Carlow. Collected by Pádraig MacDomhnaill.
85. Séamus Ó Catháin, ed. and trans., *An Hour By the Hearth: Stories Told by Pádraig Eoghain Phádraig Mac an Luain* (Dublin: University College Dublin, 1985), 32.
86. Carmichael, *Carmina Gadelica*, 1:168.
87. Ibid., 1:170.
88. Cathal Ó Searcaigh, "Here at Caiseal na gCorr Station," trans. Gabriel Fitzmaurice, in *Homecoming: Selected Poems*, ed. Gabriel Fitzmaurice (Connemara, Ireland: Có Iar-Chonnachta, 1993), 97.
89. Seamus Heaney, "The Sense of Place," in *Preoccupations: Selected Prose* (London/Boston: Faber and Faber, 1980), 131–32.
90. Ibid., 132–34.
91. Walter I. Brenneman, Jr., "Holy Wells in Ireland," in *The Power of Place and Human Environments*, ed. James A. Swan (Wheaton, Ill.: Quest Books, 1991), 137–38.
92. Lebor Gabála Érenn, *The Book of the Taking of Ireland, Part V*, ed. and trans. Robert Alexander Stewart MacAlister (Dublin: Published for Irish Texts Society by the Educational Co. of Ireland, 1956), 39.
93. Michael Dames, *Mythic Ireland* (New York/London: Thames & Hudson, 1992), 62–117.
94. Lebor Gabala Érenn, *The Book of the Taking of Ireland, Part IV*, ed. and trans. Robert Alexander Stewart MacAlister (Dublin: Published for Irish Texts Society by the Educational Co. of Ireland, 1941), 123.
95. Green, *Symbol and Image in Celtic Religious Art*, 35, 54, 58.
96. John Matthews, *Taliesin: Shamanism and the Bardic Mysteries in Britain and Ireland* (London: The Aquarian Press/HarperCollins, 1991), 14.
97. Green, *Symbol and Image in Celtic Religious Art*, 155–56.
98. Green, *Celtic Goddesses: Warriors, Virgins and Mothers*, 99–101.
99. For a fine discussion of the atmosphere of holy wells, see "Holy Wells of Ireland" by Walter I. Brenneman, Jr., in *The Power of Place and Human Environments*, ed. James A. Swan (Wheaton, Ill.: Quest Books, 1991), 135–53.
100. Peter Harbison, *Pilgrimage in Ireland: The Monuments and the People* (Syracuse, N.Y.: Syracuse University Press, 1991), 229–30.
101. Jean Markale, *The Celts: Uncovering the Mythic and Historic Origins of Western Culture* (Rochester, Vt.: Inner Traditions International, 1993), 24–25.

102. Caitlín Matthews, *Arthur and the Sovereignty of Britain: King and Goddess in the Mabinogion* (London: Arkana, 1989).
103. Lady Charlotte Guest, ed. and trans., "The Lady of the Fountain," in *The Mabinogion* (London: Bernard Quaritch, 1877/ facsimile ed. Cardiff, Wales: John Jones Cardiff, Ltd., 1977), 8.
104. Tom Peete Cross and Clark Harvis Slover, *Ancient Irish Tales* (New York: Henry Holt, 1936), 189.
105. Green, *Symbol and Image in Celtic Religious Art*, 88–89, 134–35, 164–65.
106. Elizabeth Shee Twohig, *Irish Megalithic Tombs* (Princess Risborough, Buckinghamshire, U.K.: Shire Archaeology, 1990), 12.
107. William Anderson, *Green Man: The Archetype of Our Oneness with the Earth* (London/San Francisco: HarperCollins, 1990), 40.
108. Ibid., 14–17, 64.
109. Thomas Kinsella, trans., *The Táin*, translated from the Irish epic *Táin Bó Cuailnge* (Oxford: Oxford University Press, 1969), xiv.
110. Séamus Ó Catháin, *The Festival of Brigit: Celtic Goddess and Holy Woman* (Blackrock, Co. Dublin: DBA Publications Ltd., 1995), 14.
111. Ibid., 149.
112. Séamus Mac Philib, "The Changeling," *Béaloideas* 59 (1991):121–31.
113. Ríonach Uí Ógáin, "Music Learned from the Fairies," *Béaloideas* 60–61 (1992–1993):197–214.
114. Irish Folklore Department, University College Dublin, *Main Manuscript*, 49:181–84. Told by Seán Céadagáin from Cape Clear Island, Co. Cork. Collected by Seán Standún, 1933.
115. H. M. Roe, cataloguer, *Béaloideas*, *Leoighis*, 4:34.
116. Séamus Ó Duilearga, *Seán Ó Conáill's Book: Stories and Traditions from Iveragh*, trans. Máire MacNeill (Dublin: University College, 1981).
117. Irish Folklore Department, University College Dublin, *Main Manuscript*, 744:409–10. From Aunascaul, Co. Kerry. Collected by P. J. O'Sullivan. Storyteller Bill Garvey.
118. T. Crofton Croker, *Fairy Legends and Traditions of the South of Ireland*, 1st ed. (London: John Murray, 1889). Subsequent editions were published by George Allen & Co. and did not include banshee stories.
119. Irish Folklore Department, University College Dublin, *Schools' Manuscript*, 645:70–71. From Dungarvan, Decies without Drum, Co. Waterford. Collected 1937–1938 by Seosaimhín de Paor from her mother, Bean de Paor.
120. Irish Folklore Department, University College Dublin,

Schools' Manuscript, 620:361–62. From Ballagh, Kilforora, Corcomroe, Co. Clare. Collected 1937–1938 by Terence MacMahon from Patrick MacMahon.

121. Croker, *Fairy Legends and Traditions of the South of Ireland*, 1st ed. (London: John Murray, 1889). Subsequent editions were published by George Allen & Co. and did not include banshee stories.
122. Patricia Lysaght, "The Banshee's Comb," *Béaloideas* 59 (1991):67–82.
123. Irish Folklore Department, University College Dublin, *Schools' Manuscript*, 724:121. From Moyleroe, Castletowndelvin, Delvin, Co. Westmeath. Collected 1937–1938 by Eileen O'Brien from Mrs. Gilmore.
124. Irish Folklore Department, University College Dublin, *Main Manuscript*, 1796:434–35. From Gurrawn Lower, Rathnure, Co. Wexford. Collected August–September 1973 by James G. Delaney from Patrick Leary.
125. Séan Ó hEachaidh, *Fairy Legends from Donegal*, trans. Máire MacNeill (Dublin: Comhairle Béaloideas Éireann, University College, 1977), 135.
126. Ibid., 137.
127. Ríonach Uí Ógáin, "Music Learned from the Faeries," *Béaloideas* 60–61 (1992–1993):197–214.
128. Alan Bruford, "Caught in a Fairy Dance," *Béaloideas* 62–63 (1994–1995):1–27.
129. Ríonach Uí Ógáin, "Music Learned from the Faeries," *Béaloideas* 60–61 (1992–1993):197–214.
130. Collated by Peter Kennedy and Seán Ó Baoill from Neilly Boyle, in *The Moving Clouds* (Folktracks FSA-60-170, Devon, England).
131. Robin Flower, *The Western Island or the Great Basket* (Oxford: The Clarendon Press, 1944), 116.
132. Seamus Heaney, "The Given Note," in *Door into the Dark* (London: Faber and Faber, 1969), 46.
133. Séamus Ó Catháin, *Béaloideas* 59 (1991):145–59.
134. Folklore of Ireland Society, Recorded by Séamus Ó Catháin from John Henry, Erris, Co. Mayo, on June 4, 1989, *Béaloideas* 59 (1991):146.
135. William Butler Yeats, "The Ballad of Father Gilligan," in *The Celtic Twilight and a Selection of Early Poems* (New York: New American Library, Signet Classic by arrangement with Macmillan Co., 1962), 185–86.
136. Carmichael, *Carmina Gadelica*, 1:xxiii–xxix.
137. John Matthews, *Taliesin: Shamanism and the Bardic Mysteries in Britain and Ireland*

(London: The Aquarian Press/ HarperCollins, 1991), 3–4, 127–47.

138. John and Caitlín Matthews, "Primary Chief Bard," quoted in *Taliesin: Shamanism and the Bardic Mysteries in Britain and Ireland* (London: The Aquarian Press/ HarperCollins, 1991), 283–85.
139. Carmichael, *Carmina Gadelica*, 1:xxi.
140. Ibid., 6–7.
141. Ibid., 60–61.
142. Walter L. Brenneman, Jr., "Holy Wells of Ireland," in *The Power of Place and Human Environments*, ed. James A. Swan (Wheaton, Ill.: Quest Books, 1991), 138–40.
143. Carmichael, *Carmina Gadelica*, 1:204.
144. Ibid., 3:285.
145. Ibid., 1:122.
146. Ibid., 3:285.
147. Green, *Symbol and Image in Celtic Religious Art*, 103–4.
148. Green, *Animals in Celtic Life and Myth*, 214–15.
149. Green, *Symbol and Image in Celtic Religious Art*, 46–54, 74–86.
150. Green, *Celtic Myths*, 15–16.
151. Green, *Symbol and Image in Celtic Religious Art*, 74–86.
152. Ibid., 211–12.
153. Green, *Celtic Myths*, 71.
154. Patrick K. Ford, trans. and ed., *The Mabinogion and Other Medieval Welsh Tales* (Berkeley/ Los Angeles/London: University of California Press, 1977), 70.
155. Green, *Symbol and Image in Celtic Religious Art*, 164–65.
156. Ibid., 39.
157. Ibid., 23.
158. Ibid., 116–28.
159. Green, *Celtic Myths* (London/Austin, Texas: British Museum Press/University of Texas Press, 1993), 46–47.
160. Irish Folklore Department, University College Dublin, *Main Manuscript*, 117:114. Collected by S. P. Ó Piotáin from Mrs. Anne Gavaghan, Cloonfinish, Swinford, Co. Mayo, in 1935.
161. Green, *Celtic Myths*, 49.
162. Lucan, *Pharsalia*, trans. Jane Wilson Joyce (Ithaca, N.Y./London: Cornell University Press, 1993), 302.
163. For one of many versions, see David H. Green, "The Dream of Oenghus," in *An Anthology of Irish Literature* (New York: The Modern Library, 1954), 39–43.
164. Ford, *The Mabinogion and Other Medieval Welsh Tales*, 119–58.
165. Heaney, *Over Nine Waves: A Book of Irish Legends*, 15.
166. Ibid., 3–21.
167. Ibid.
168. Ibid., 58.
169. Julius Caesar, *De Bello Gallico*, *IV*, ed. E. C. Kennedy (Bristol, U.K.: Bristol Classical Press, 1967/1982), 24–33.
170. Thomas Kinsella, trans., *The Táin*, translated from the Irish

epic *Táin Bó Cuailnge* (Oxford: Oxford University Press, 1969), 147, 153.

171. Lebor Gabála Érenn, *The Book of the Taking of Ireland, Part V*, ed. and trans. Robert Alexander Stewart MacAlister (Dublin: Published for Irish Texts Society by the Educational Co. of Ireland, 1956), 107.
172. Ibid., 175.
173. Green, *Symbol and Image in Celtic Religious Art*, 116.
174. Green, *Celtic Myths*, 45–47.
175. Green, *Symbol and Image in Celtic Religious Art*, 38–39.
176. Kathleen Raine, "Iona," in *Celtic Christianity: Ecology and Holiness* (Hudson, N.Y.: Lindisfarne Press, 1982), 139.
177. Heaney, *Over Nine Waves: A Book of Irish Legends*, 57.
178. Kuno Meyer, trans., "The Isles of the Happy," in *Ancient Irish Poetry* (London: Constable, 1913/1994), 3–4.
179. Heaney, *Over Nine Waves: A Book of Irish Legends*, 216.

PERMISSIONS

The author acknowledges occasional spelling variations in Gaelic names between the text and the quoted material.

Grateful acknowledgment is made to the following for permission to reprint previously published material:

Cló Iar-Chonnachta Teo and Cathal Ó Searcaigh: Excerpt from "Mountain Woman" by Cathal Ó Searcaigh, translated by Lillis Ó Laiore, in *Homecoming: Selected Poems*, edited by Gabriel Fitzmaurice, copyright © 1993 by Cathal Ó Searcaigh (Cló Iar-Chonnachta Teo, Indreabhán, Ireland). Reprinted by kind permission of Cló Iar-Chonnachta Teo and Cathal Ó Searcaigh.

Constable Publishers: Excerpt from "The Isles of the Happy," translated by Kuno Meyer, in *Ancient Irish Poetry*. First published in 1913 and reprinted in 1994 by Constable Publishers, London. Reprinted by kind permission of Constable Publishers.

Department of Irish Folklore, National University of Ireland, Dublin: Excerpts from the *Main Manuscript* and *Schools' Manuscript* archives. Reprinted by kind permission of the Head of the Department of Irish Folklore, National University of Ireland, Dublin.

Faber and Faber Limited and Seamus Heaney: Excerpt from *Over Nine Waves: A Book of Irish Legends* by Marie Heaney, copyright © 1994 by Marie Heaney (Faber and Faber, London/Boston). Reprinted by kind permission of Faber and Faber Limited. "The Given Note" in *Door into the Dark*, copyright © 1969 by Seamus Heaney (Faber and Faber, London). Reprinted by kind permission of Faber and Faber Limited and Seamus Heaney.

Farrar, Straus & Giroux, Inc., and Carcanet Press Limited: Excerpt from *The White Goddess: A Historical Grammar of Poetic Myth* by Robert Graves, copyright © 1948 and renewed in 1975 by Robert Graves (Farrar, Straus & Giroux, Inc., New York, 1948). Rights outside of the United States, its dependencies, and the Philippines administered by Carcanet Press Limited, Manchester, England. Reprinted by kind permission of Farrar, Straus & Giroux, Inc., and Carcanet Press Limited.

Permissions

Folklore of Ireland Council: Excerpt from *An Hour by the Hearth: Stories Told by Pádraig Eoghain Phádraig Mac an Luain* by Séamas Ó Catháin, copyright © 1985 by Séamas Ó Catháin (University College Dublin). Reprinted by kind permission of the Folklore of Ireland Council and Séamas Ó Catháin.

Folklore of Ireland Society: Excerpt from *Béaloideas*, vol. 59, 1991, p. 146. Reprinted by kind permission of the Folklore of Ireland Society and Séamus Ó Catháin.

HarperCollins Publishers: Excerpts from "The Consolation of Elffin," "Gad Goddeu," and "Primary Chief Bard," translated by John and Caitlín Matthews, in *Taliesin: Shamanism and the Bardic Mysteries in Britain and Ireland* by John Matthews, copyright © 1991 by John Matthews (The Aquarian Press/HarperCollins, London). Reprinted by kind permission of HarperCollins Publishers, London.

Henry Holt and Company, Inc.: Excerpts from *Ancient Irish Tales* by Tom Peete Cross and Clark Harris Slover, copyright © 1936 by Tom Peete Cross and Clark Harris Slover (Henry Holt, New York). Reprinted by kind permission of Henry Holt and Company, Inc.

Irish Texts Society: Excerpt from *Cath Maig Tired: The Second Battle of Mag Tuired*, edited by Elizabeth A. Gray, copyright © 1982 by Elizabeth A. Gray (Irish Texts Society, London). Reprinted by kind permission of the Irish Texts Society.

New Island Books/Raven Arts Press and Nuala Ní Dhomhnaill: "Mór Hatching" and "Donncha Dí's Testimony" in *Selected Poems*, copyright © 1986, 1988 by Nuala Ní Dhomhnaill and translated by Michael Hartnett (New Island Books/Raven Arts Press, Dublin). Reprinted by kind permission of New Island Books/Raven Arts Press and Nuala Ní Dhomhnaill.

Scottish Academic Press: Excerpts from *Carmina Gadelica: Hymns and Incantations with Illustrative Notes on Words, Rites, and Customs, Dying and Obsolete: Orally Collected in the Highlands and Islands of Scotland and Translated into English* by Alexander Carmichael (Scottish Academic Press, Edinburgh, vols. I–VI). Reprinted by kind permission of the Trustees.

Simon & Schuster Publishers and A.P. Watt Limited: Excerpt from "The Ballad of Father Gilligan," in *The Celtic Twilight and a Selection of Early Poems* by William Butler Yeats, published by Signet Classics by arrangement with The Macmillan Company, 1962. Rights outside of the United States, its dependencies, and the Philippines administered by A.P. Watt Limited, London, on behalf of Michael Yeats. Reprinted by kind permission of Simon & Schuster Publishers and A.P. Watt Limited.

ORACLES INDEX